W9-CQT-165

A Responsible Life
The Spiritual Path of Mussar

A Responsible Life

The Spiritual Path of Mussar

IRA F. STONE

AVIV PRESS

NEW YORK

Copyright © 2006   Ira F. Stone

All rights reserved. No part of the text may be reproduced in any form, nor may any page be photographed and reproduced, without the written permission of the publisher.

Translations from *Siddur Sim Shalom for Shabbat and Festivals* © 1998, the Rabbinical Assembly. Reprinted by permission of the Rabbinical Assembly.

Library of Congress Cataloging-in-Publication Data

Stone, Ira F.
    A responsible life : the spiritual path of mussar / by Ira F. Stone.
        p. cm.
    Includes bibliographical references.
    ISBN-13 978-0-916219-31-4 (alk. paper)
    1. Mussar movement.   2. Jewish ethics.   3. Jewish way of life.   4. Judaism—Doctrines.   I. Title.

  BJ1285.5.M8S76 2006
  296.3'4—dc22   2006013682

Published by Aviv Press
An imprint of the Rabbinical Assembly
3080 Broadway, New York, NY 10027

Cover design by Jennifer Klor

Printed in the United States of America

*This book has been generously sponsored
by the following donors:*

──────── ◻ ────────

In memory of two beautiful women

Blanche Newman and Eleanor Sands

JUDY SANDS NEWMAN & BUD NEWMAN

◻ ◻ ◻

In honor of a great teacher and friend

HARRIS, DEBBIE, ELIZABETH, AND RACHEL DEVOR

◻ ◻ ◻

SALEM D. SHUCHMAN AND BARBARA L. KLOCK FAMILY FOUNDATION

"I am responsible for the Other without waiting for reciprocity.

It is I who support all. The I always has one responsibility more than all the others."

—EMMANUEL LEVINAS

In honor of our teacher, Rabbi Stone

Through his teachings and his actions, he has shown each of us the path toward a more conscious and compassionate life.

SUSAN BALIS • ERIC BERGER • JOSHUA BOETTIGER • ALLISON CARTER
JIM CULBERTSON • NANCY FUCHS KREIMER • RICHARD MANDEL
JOYCE NORDEN • MICHAEL A. POSNER • ROBERT RUBIN
ANDREW SELIGMAN • MINDY SHAPIRO • JOANNA SARAH SLUSKY
EUGENE SOTIRESCU • BEULAH TREY • MICHAEL VOGEL • SONIA VOYNOW
BILL WEISMAN • LEAH WEISMAN • MATTHEW WHITEHORN
MIKI YOUNG • ROBERT ZIMRING

In Memory of Emmanuel Levinas

The word I means *here I am,*
answering for everything and for everyone.

—*Otherwise than Being and Beyond Essence*

Contents

PART FOUR ▣ *Mussar* and *Mitzvot*

APPENDIX

Acknowledgments

I have been at work on this book in different ways over the course of many years. I want to thank some of the people who have contributed to this work finally coming together.

Without Lane Gerber I would not have been introduced to Emmanuel Levinas's work and without Annette Aronowicz I would not have begun to understand it. I am grateful to both. Without Rabbi Dov Bard I wouldn't have had anyone to talk to about *Mesillat Yesharim*. For over thirty years we have pursued the path together at a distance. He is my *hevruta* par excellence. I am very grateful for the support and friendship of Rabbi Martin Samuel Cohen. His constant encouragement of my work and our mutual commitment and belief that one can be a contemporary Conservative rabbi and maintain an active spiritual and intellectual life have been a blessing.

Most directly responsible for this book are Amy Gottlieb, Director of Publications for the Rabbinical Assembly and Aviv Press, and Elisheva Urbas and Michelle Kwitkin-Close, my editors. Their joint vision for what this book could be, rather than what it was when I gave it to them, was truly inspiring. They have given much of themselves for this other.

I would like to acknowledge the assistance of my students over the years at the Jewish Theological Seminary, where I have taught in the department of Jewish Philosophy. My course, "Introduction to the Literature of the Mussar Movement," produced many discussions that enriched this volume. Specifically I want to thank Rachel Sabath-Beit Halachmi, Jeremy Wiederhorn, and Alain Dreshner for the preliminary translations and commentaries they did of some chapters in Ḥokhmah U-Mussar. Their efforts were helpful guides for my work.

I want to thank the officers and members of Temple Beth Zion–Beth Israel in Philadelphia, where I am rabbi, for their unstinting support and interest in my work. In this regard, the staff of BZBI has been constantly supportive. I would like to offer a special thank you to Cantor George Mordechai; Donna Rosenthal, our Executive Director; and my administrative assistant, Phyllis Kramer, for providing an inspiring work environment.

I am especially grateful to the students of the Philadelphia Mussar Institute. Over the past three years they have demonstrated an uncommon commitment to the vision of spiritual growth and ethical responsibility that I have been trying to discover and to teach. Their trust has been a gift.

The final work on this book was done during my stay at Harvard University as the Rabbi Daniel Jeremy Silver Rabbinic Fellow. I am grateful to the faculty and staff of the Center for Jewish Studies at Harvard for their hospitality.

I want to especially thank my family. My wife Annie continues to be my primary instructor in Mussar. I owe her more than I can say. Our children—Tamar and Alan, Yoshi, and Shuli—have given me their unwavering love from their youngest years until the present, teaching me to pay close attention to the interruptions that make life worth living. I undertook the bulk of the writing of this book, after years of study and collecting notes, in the weeks before Tamar and Alan's wedding. Without the need to find some escape from the pressures of those preparations I may never have been motivated to get to work. I am grateful.

I am always grateful for each breath of life vouchsafed me by the Holy One of Israel, *barukh hu u-varukh shemo.*

Ira F. Stone

April 2006/Nisan 5766

Philadelphia

Introduction

What prevents me from doing what is good? If I know what is right, if I espouse a set of values that describe the good, why is it so difficult to act on that knowledge and those values? Faced with a world where there is so much evil, what can I really do to make a difference? These are questions that most of us ask ourselves at one time or another. Sometimes we ask ourselves these questions because we are disappointed with how we've acted in a particular situation, such as when we've turned down an opportunity to help someone because it was inconvenient or uncomfortable (for example, passing a panhandler on the street). Sometimes these questions occur to us because our involvement in various activities suggests it ought to be easier, or perhaps more natural, for us to be the kind of people we want to be—and yet we still seem to fall short of our aspirations, never fully living up to the ideals enshrined in our deepest values. For example, while working in a hospital or nursing home, we might feel resentful when a patient or resident makes a demand upon us. Or we may be very involved in the life of our religious community, and yet still experience an unsettling "disconnect" between the rituals we practice and the texts we learn, on the one hand, and the people we'd like to be, whose actions exemplify the values we hold dear, on the other hand.

This is neither a new or unusual phenomenon. It is not

unusual in that the compromises we make with our ideals are compromises that people make all the time. It is not new in that, at least within the Jewish tradition, an entire literature and school of thought has addressed these questions before us. Both that literature and that movement are called Mussar. "Mussar" means "correction," or "instruction" in the sense of correction (like the English word "discipline," which refers not only to corrective measures but more generally to the pedagogic objectives the corrections seek to achieve). However, "Mussar" has come to signify moral education more generally, and it is the simple Hebrew word for ethics and morals. As a literature, Mussar can be said to extend back to the exhortations of the biblical prophets and biblical wisdom literature (such as the Book of Proverbs). More specifically, it describes a genre of spiritual-ethical exhortation that emerged in the tenth century and has continued to grow to our own time. The Mussar movement developed primarily in Lithuania in the second half of the nineteenth century. Founded by Rabbi Israel Lipkin of Salant, it sought to explore the composition of the human soul and provide a series of techniques to help minimize the "disconnect" so often experienced between our actions and our ideals.

If the questions with which we began resonate for us, then Mussar can provide a structure for beginning to address them. It demands that our day-to-day actions be suffused with a concern for doing the good. It also demands that the good that we do be grounded in communal norms and obligations, rather than left to the whims of the individual. Mussar grows out of the soil of Jewish experience. It was, and continues to be, shaped by the central pillars of Jewish consciousness: Torah and *mitzvot*. Mussar takes for granted immersion in Torah and is, at its core, inseparable from this traditional Jewish context. There is much that one who does not share these commitments can learn from the theory and practice of Mussar, but it will be most meaningful to the committed Jew.

Different people will be enriched by Mussar in different ways. It might deepen one person's experience of Jewish ritual, challenging them to uncover the values at the core of that ritual. It might draw another person closer to an understanding of the purpose of Jewish ritual, challenging the notion that the limits of one's responsibility are defined by each of us for ourselves. This book is intended for all such seekers.

I first became interested in Mussar as a beginning rabbinic student. I had come to the seminary after a short but intense career as a social activist. Called to conscience by the Civil Rights movement of the 1960s, I worked for a time in that movement, specifically agitating for fair housing policies in New York City. Later I became active in the student movements of the time and was a participant in the demonstrations against the war in Vietnam. During this time and prior to enrolling in the Seminary I had been a street outreach worker among teenage drug abusers. The concern to carry my social consciousness into the fabric of my religious commitments was self-evident to me. This concern deepened as I soon learned that the two commitments did not always go together. I learned that the beauty of the ritual practice I had come to love was often seen as an end in itself, rather than as a context for doing good. My discovery of Mussar was both discouraging and encouraging. It was discouraging, in that it meant that *mitzvot* (namely, Jewish religious observance) and *middot* (ethical self-discipline) did not always go together. It was encouraging, in that it provided a methodology within the tradition for addressing this fact.

Integrating Mussar theory and practice into my life and my religious observance was impeded by the fact that the traditional Mussar texts grew out of a Jewish theology that was problematic for me. The ideas that these texts espoused about God, reward and punishment, life after death—not to mention their essentially fundamentalist view of sacred Scripture—were at odds with my post-

Holocaust, post–Enlightenment sensibilities. But Mussar remained in the back of my mind as a spiritual option that I wanted to explore.

Emmanuel Levinas: A Modern Jewish Thinker

I spent a great deal of my intellectual energy over the course of the next twenty years as a rabbi in two congregations trying to find a theology that was both compelling in itself for a post-Holocaust, post-Enlightenment Jew and would also support a practice modeled on Mussar teachings. The culmination of that search for me was the discovery of the work of the French-Jewish philosopher Emmanuel Levinas. Levinas's thought has only recently entered into the world of the rabbinic seminary, and still rather marginally—even as his import as a thinker has become widely celebrated in the academic world. Levinas, who came from Lithuania and lived his early years in the shadow of the height of the Mussar movement's influence over Lithuanian Jewry, was born in Kovno in 1906. His parents were "enlightened" Jews of the time. His father was a bookseller and Levinas was given the best secular education available to a Jew at the time. He was privately tutored in Jewish studies and cites Bible and Hebrew as having constituted the core of his Jewish education. Levinas left Lithuania in 1923 in order to study in Strasbourg, France. He never returned. In 1928 he became a student of two of the most important philosophers of the twentieth century, Edmund Husserl and Martin Heidegger. Under their influence, and in critical dialogue with them, Levinas began to create his own philosophic system in the late 1930s.

Tragically, Levinas spent the war years as a French prisoner of war in a Nazi labor camp, while his wife and infant daughter were hidden in a French monastery. Both his wife's and his own parents, and the rest of their extended family in Lithuania, were murdered. The profound effect of these events found powerful expression in his later writings, which explored the philosophical roots of political totalitarianism.

After the war Levinas continued to develop his earlier thought with renewed urgency. At the same time he turned to a serious study of Talmud. While he had not studied Talmud as a youngster, he began to study it with a rather unique and mysterious figure in post-war France called Monsieur Shoshani. Monsieur Shoshani has been described in more detail by Elie Wiesel in his autobiography, *All the Rivers Run to the Sea*. Levinas integrated insights from his philosophical work into his talmudic studies and vice versa. In addition to publishing a number of the most demanding and important works of twentieth-century philosophy, Levinas also published a series of talmudic commentaries as well as important essays on other areas of Jewish thought. Full descriptions of either his philosophy or his Jewish writings are beyond the scope of this book. However, the relevance of Levinas's ideas to my growing interest in Mussar is not.

Levinas's thought emphasizes not the primacy of the self, but the primacy of the other—that is, other human beings. He taught that the self comes into existence by virtue of the other; therefore, the self comes into being indebted to the other. This other, the other person, is presented to the individual through a face-to-face encounter that commands a response in action. For Levinas, this face-to-face encounter shatters the self-containedness or insularity of the self. Therefore a philosophy that begins with this intersubjective encounter can shatter the totalitarianism implicit in Western philosophy. In other words, questions of ethics precede questions of being. To put it another way, the question "What is being?" is asked only after we ask the question "What is my responsibility in being?" Western philosophy has been nearly obsessed with the question of being, while relegating the question of ethics to a secondary role. Levinas strongly suggests that the political atrocities of the last century derive from this misplaced emphasis. More importantly, an ethics that begins by recognizing our obligations to others as prior even to those obligations we have to ourselves suggested to me the same radical power I had always suspected in Mussar.

Emmanuel Levinas's philosophy has been formative for my own theology. For Levinas, God is able to re-enter the post-Holocaust discourse as a command. For him, it is blasphemous to conceive of a God limited to the arena of being—that is, the world that is comprehensible to us in thought and language. Worse, any attempt to foist onto God the responsibility for the vicissitudes of our lives—let alone the culpability for the tragic events of the twentieth century—is an even more blasphemous evasion of our own responsibility. The grandeur of Jewish thought thus lies in its *hutzpah* in assigning responsibility for others to humans, both individually and collectively. God, for Levinas, is not a presence but an absence. That absence is not simply emptiness, but rather a trace of God—God's "back," if you will, alluding to Exodus 34:6, a favorite biblical passage for Levinas. That text describes the inability of Moses (and hence of any human being) to "see" (i.e., to comprehend) God. Instead, God offers to Moses a vision of God's back in passing: "Adonai passed by before him and proclaimed: Adonai, Adonai, mighty, merciful and gracious, longsuffering, and abundant in love and truth, keeping truth to thousands, forgiving iniquity and transgression and sin, but who will by no means clear the guilty . . ." Levinas locates this trace of God on the face of the other person. The face of the other is not the face of God, but rather it is the place of the *trace* of God's having passed by, thereby leaving us responsible. For Levinas, to be "chosen" or "commanded," two essential Jewish theological terms, means to recognize and act on this commanded responsibility vis-à-vis the other person.

This philosophic program, with its emphasis on responsibility for the other, turned my attention back to Mussar with a clearer understanding of what I could mean when I used words like "God" or "*mitzvah.*"

As a result of finding a theological comfort zone by way of Levinas's philosophy, I was able to turn back to Mussar texts and begin to envision a contemporary Mussar practice. The writings of Rav Yisrael Salanter were a starting-point, as were other classical Mussar texts that preceded the Mussar movement per se. Most important in this regard is *Mesillat Yesharim* by Rabbi Moshe Hayyim Luzzatto. These and other Mussar texts will figure in our description of both the theory and practice of contemporary Mussar. However, one set of writings stands out for its impact on the development of my thinking and practice of Mussar. That is the work *Hokhmah U-Mussar* by Rabbi Simha Zissel Braude of Kelm, who was one of the three primary students of Rav Yisrael Salanter, each of whom established a school of Mussar: Rabbi Nathan Zvi Finkel founded the Slobadka school, Rabbi Joseph Yozel Hurwitz founded the Navaradock school, and Rabbi Simha Zissel Braude founded the Kelm school. These were all traditional *yeshivot,* with the usual Torah curriculum, but they also included an emphasis on Mussar. Each was a "school" in that it followed the particular philosophic and pedagogic principles of its founder, although all were ultimately based on the ideas of Rav Yisrael Salanter.

Philosophy of Mussar

Rav Yisrael Salanter was the founder of the Mussar movement in the nineteenth century and several of his key ideas have been crucial for the development of my own thought. First and foremost, Salanter believed that Mussar—the quest for ethical perfection—is a process. In addition, he taught that this process encounters opposition from our personalities, since the very traits that are required to establish our individual identities impede this quest. Therefore, Salanter's educational goal is to transform personality or human nature. Critical to Salanter's Mussar is the idea that service to and responsibility for other human beings is the single most important human value.

As radical as the theory of Mussar that Rabbi Salanter propounded was, its method was considered even more radical. He dared, first of all, to raise the study of traditional Mussar texts (such as the tenth-century *Duties of the Heart* and the eighteenth-century *Path of the Upright*) to a level just below that of the study of Talmud. In Jewish Lithuania this was revolutionary. Texts that had been regarded as ancillary, exhortative, and useful only to the weak-minded were raised to the highest imaginable levels on the basis of the fact that the message of these texts had not yet been mastered by even accomplished scholars. Mussar texts, according to Salanter, were to be studied daily just as legal texts were: in groups, aloud, and with passion and intensity. Rav Salanter used the methods that had succeeded so well in developing a culture of extraordinary erudition in attempting to create a culture of equally extraordinary ethical behavior.

However, since the goal was to transform behavior, more was necessary than simply book-learning. Behavior had to be monitored, and the impediments to changing behavior that are deeply rooted in people's personalities had to be addressed. Salanter's method was based on an implicit understanding of the forces "unconsciously" at work on human beings; just as startling as Freud's theory was, Salanter's method also required, like Freud, a type of therapeutic talking. This was to include first a talking to oneself, and then the dynamics of what can only be called group analysis. Salanter called for students to sequester themselves for a period of time every day, and to use this time to review (aloud and passionately) the values found in the Mussar texts. Students were to utilize a behavioral checklist with which to measure their progress or lack thereof. In addition, Salanter created Mussar groups in which individuals would gently point out ethical failures among the members and then, just as gently, help them find the strength to change such behaviors. The most important method of correction was called *hitpa'alut*. This means "self-work" and refers to a process by which the student would search through traditional texts for statements that addressed the particular character trait being worked on. The student was urged to memorize such statements and to have them at hand when confronting situations where the character trait was in play. If, for example, I were tempted to falsely value myself and lose sight of the ethical importance of humility, then I should repeat to myself a statement such as this one from Pirke Avot: "Whoever seeks fame, destroys one's own name." This could remind me (or, more importantly, my subconscious mind) of all the hard work and difficult introspection in which I had already engaged, in order to come to terms with my real worth in the world and leave behind the need for false worth. To put it simply, Salanter believed that the process of transforming ourselves into ethical, responsible beings was too difficult and too important to leave to happenstance. It required active effort.

Simḥa Zissel and the Mussar Movement

Simḥa Zissel was born into a prominent rabbinic family in Kelm in 1829, and he received a thorough traditional education in the Lithuanian mode—and, uncharacteristically, a substantial general education as well. His Jewish education consisted of Bible studies as a boy, followed primarily by Talmud studies. The program of study most prevalent in Lithuanian *yeshivot* at that time included mastering Jewish legal norms and acquiring the skills for making halakhic (i.e., rabbinic legal) decisions, but it also focused intensely on the skills to enable the student to engage in the minute dialectic known as *pilpul*. Rav Simḥa was also, no doubt, initiated into the secrets of Kabbalah—not the ecstatic mysticism of the Ḥasidim, but the contemplative mystical tradition of the Gaon of Vilna and Rabbi Ḥayyim of Volozhin.

Recognized early as a gifted student, Simḥa Zissel left his own teachers and their rigorous program of study to investigate the growing popularity of Rav Yisrael Salanter and his Mussar teaching. Initially he approached this new movement skeptically, or so he later claimed, but upon hearing Salanter speak he decided to stay the year studying with him. He never left the movement, becoming a life-long adherent of Mussar. Simḥa Zissel's embrace of Mussar study must have mirrored the same factors that attracted so many other young Torah students to the Mussar movement. Buffeted by the *Haskalah* (Enlightenment) among the Jews of Russia, he must have been sympathetic to the enlighteners' critique that *pilpul* and rote observance of Jewish law had dried the soul of Jewish culture. Certainly, a spiritually sensitive young man might have viewed the burgher Jewish establishment with some suspicion. In any case, Salanter's message of ethical renewal captivated Simḥa Zissel, who was soon to become one of its ablest spokesmen. Moreover, he would become a prime architect of its pedagogy, with its revolutionary emphasis on general education in addition to Mussar and Torah.

The relationship between Yisrael Salanter and Simḥa Zissel soon flourished. Simḥa Zissel became one of Salanter's closest confidants. Salanter left Russia in 1857 for Prussia—at first for health reasons, but he eventually settled there to continue building his movement. Simḥa Zissel, however, remained to establish the institutional framework to perpetuate Salanter's ideas and methods. Simḥa Zissel's outstanding administrative skills combined with his Torah scholarship, kabbalistic wisdom, familiarity with general education, and extraordinary personal ethical qualities—his *menschlikheit*—enabled him to reach beyond his teacher's modest beginnings in establishing a Mussar school.

Initially, Rav Simḥa Zissel established Mussar houses in both Kovno and Vilna. These were primarily for lay people, both adult men and women, and laid the foundation for the widespread popular success of the movement. He based his program on the ideas originally put forward by Rav Salanter: that one's education ought to include the study of Talmud, the study of Mussar texts with passionate intensity, the use of peer-groups to scrutinize and improve the student's ethical posture, and a general educational program. For Rav Salanter, the openness to secular education was considered necessary in order to understand and refute the adherents of the *Haskalah*. However, Rav Simḥa Zissel went even further, considering all knowledge (even of secular subjects) to be sacred and therefore appropriate for Jews to study. His outlook more closely resembled the view of the *Haskalah* itself. He believed that knowledge of the workings of the world, particularly of science, would result in a heightened appreciation of God's handiwork—and such intellectual pursuits were therefore to be encouraged. The fact that he quotes Aristotle in his own work indicates that the scope of this education went beyond the merely practical. This was a significant shift from the accepted Orthodoxy of his time.

In 1874, Rabbi Simḥa Zissel returned to Kelm after many years in Kovno and established a *yeshiva* there called Bet Ha-talmud. The *yeshiva* moved from Kelm to nearby Grobin in 1876 because of growing opposition from the Kelm Jewish establishment to Rav Simḥa Zissel's innovations, in both the curriculum and in religious practice. On Shabbat, for example, contrary to traditional Jewish practice, the *yeshiva* community would conclude the morning service *(Shaḥarit)* and take their lunch before returning for the additional *(Musaf)* service, followed by a session of Mussar study. Many townspeople in Kelm thought that too much time was being spent on Mussar, to the detriment of Talmud study. There was also growing harassment from the Tsarist government, in response to what they deemed revolutionary activity in the *yeshiva*. Rav Simḥa actively attempted to provide religious succor to the many young Jews conscripted into the Tsar's army (often for up to twenty-five years); it is also likely that students were hidden from conscription in one way or another. The *yeshiva*'s involvement in these efforts led to growing government threats to close its doors.

The *yeshiva* in Grobin was the crowning achievement of Simḥa Zissel's life and the leading Mussar center of its time; its influence spread throughout Russia and reached even as far as Palestine. Rav Simḥa left the *yeshiva* in 1886 because of ill health, itself a consequence of his dedication to the school and the movement, and he died in 1898. The *yeshiva* continued as an important center of Mussar until the Nazis destroyed it, together with its teachers and students, during World War II. However, the legacy of Kelm's Mussar school survived the war, primarily in the community of Gateshead in England as well as at various *yeshivot* in Israel. Although Mussar has survived in all of its forms (and continues to flourish even today within the Ḥaredi, or so-called ultra-Orthodox, community), it is the methods of the Kelm School that are fundamental to the contemporary Mussar I practice—in no small measure because in Rav Simḥa's work we find an authentic, traditional expression of ideas, which I had taken from Levinas. The thematic and linguistic similarities between Levinasian ethical thought and the Mussar of Rav Simḥa Zissel brought me full circle.

In the opening chapter of *Ḥokhmah U-Mussar* Rav Simḥa writes:

> Our Sages taught: One of the methods by which the Torah is acquired is by carrying the burden with our fellow. Each of the [48] steps which they enumerate there [Avot 6] are like preliminary goals, achieved by following each step, in order to bring about the ultimate goal. All of them taken together instill in one a new nature—that of being "Master of a fine soul." One then becomes fit for Torah and wisdom to be attached to, as a result of which one's soul is bound up with the bond of eternal life. Without this it is impossible to acquire Torah, for it is a spiritual entity and cannot attach itself to one who does not merit it on account of one's continuing pre-occupation with material matters.

Rav Simḥa begins his essay by focusing on one of the forty-eight personality qualities *(middot)* that Pirke Avot sees as necessary for one to "acquire" Torah (i.e., binding the spiritual force of Torah to the human soul). It is a common Jewish mystical notion that the physical Torah is but a "cover" for a spiritual (or supernal) Torah: the literal Torah "hides" a more purely spiritual vehicle. Simḥa's reading of Avot is no more literal than his understanding of the Torah. Although Avot seems to consider these *middot* as all equally important, Rav Simḥa claims that "carrying the burden with one's fellow" is the goal of all the rest; reaching this goal testifies to the transformation of one's human nature into a spiritual nature, transcending even death itself. It is to this transformed infinite soul, whose infinity is effected by bearing the pain of others, that the spiritual Torah adheres.

This description of Torah implies that the relationship between the enclosed self and the other person bridges the gap between the finite and infinite, between each of us and God, by our assuming responsibility one for another. The introduction of infinity, or eternity, into this equation, though not unexpected in a religious document, is effected by the reference to eternal life and suggests an obligation toward the other that precedes the self. In a very real sense then, the Torah is only brought into the world by bearing the burden of the other. Simultaneously, the soul itself comes into being by attaching itself to this Torah, which itself came into existence by virtue of bearing the burden of the other. Creation of the individual as a physical being (a given in this world) is thus transformed by Torah—what we can already call revelation, which we can understand as a command to guide us toward redemption. This must be redemption not of ourselves but of the other, whose burden we bear.

In the writings of Rav Simḥa Zissel, then, we find a Jewish theology and the theoretical basis for a Jewish practice that seems to anticipate the philosophy of Emmanuel Levinas. The key terms of Jewish theology—creation, revelation, and redemption—are understood as functions of how we behave toward our neighbor, how we help them bear the burdens of life. The literal language describing God, revelation, eternity, and redemption that had been the theological impediment to my considering Mussar practice in a contemporary milieu was thus doubly lifted. The impact of Kelm and Levinas taken together led me to develop my own working theology of contemporary Mussar.

The Fate of Mussar

Salanter's Mussar movement did not gain the approval of established authorities in the Jewish community either inside or outside the *yeshiva*. Inside the *yeshiva* world, this was because he challenged the hegemony of Talmud study and its powerful rabbinic hierarchy. Outside the *yeshiva* world, this was because he challenged the ethical standards of the entire community. Salanter was forced, at various times, to leave Vilna, Kovno, and other cities. Since he believed his movement was needed not only in Lithuania, he also traveled to Germany, France, and England to attempt to spread his doctrine. In fact, teaching Mussar became one of the methods available to students of Mussar for perfecting their *middot,* since teaching is an act of taking responsibility for another.

The Mussar movement was attractive to many students of Torah, and to many lay people in the Jewish community as well, due to a variety of complex factors. Among Western Jews, especially in Lithuania, the century-old enthusiasm for Ḥasidism had not spread. Its simple, ecstatic, almost superstitious mysticism had found no home among the more intellectually conditioned communities, and its influence remained largely confined to Eastern Europe. Yet, these intellectual communities still yearned for some renewed passion, which Mussar provided. Moreover these communities were, at the time, heavily impacted by the growth of the Jewish Enlightenment. Salanter was pre-eminently a child of his century and Mussar contained elements that attracted many who were not prepared to abandon Judaism, but for whom ideas from the Enlightenment (such as individualism, individual responsibility, and the unconscious) were attractive. Salanter legitimized the teaching of secular studies in the *yeshiva* and this was similarly attractive. For Salanter, ostensibly, this was encouraged in order for Mussar followers to be familiar enough with Enlightenment thought to combat it. In practice, of course, it served to introduce many in the *yeshivot* to those ideas in a relatively safe and secure environment.

None of this should obscure Rav Salanter's dedication to the simple but profound ideal that the goal of human life was love of one's neighbor; all of human misery derived from our inability to manage such a love. Salanter's chief student, Rav Simḥa Zissel Braude of Kelm, advanced this commitment to the overwhelming centrality of the love of the other and the responsibilities attendant on such love.

The Necessity of Mussar

Why do I find Mussar so compelling, that I have invested years in clearing the theological ground beneath it? The survival of the Jewish people and their culture is due to many factors, but one must not underestimate the power of binding law to undergird the development of that culture, its religion, philosophy, and literature. Law and culture have been inseparable in Jewish thinking from its earliest beginnings. Certainly the Jewish life that took shape after the destruction of the Temple in Jerusalem and the loss of Jewish political identity, what we call the Judaism of the Mishnah and Talmud or Rabbinic Judaism, is characterized by its intense and devoted study of and observance of Jewish law *(halakhah)*. The Bible also quite clearly places adherence to legal norms at the center of its religious worldview. Israel is conceived as a covenantal people, a people constituted by its adherence to a divine commandment.

This commitment to law was implicitly understood to have purpose. From the point of view of God, it established or restored some kind of original balance to the whole of creation. And from the point of view of humanity, it perfected the human personality shaped in the image of God. In both the Bible itself and the commentaries and legal codes that grew from it, this purpose is taken for granted.

This emphasis on law, while a crucial factor in the survival of Judaism and part of its genius, is equally responsible for one of its oft-recurring flaws: the narrowing of focus from the *purpose* of the law to the *means* of achieving that purpose. At times, the study and practice of law (especially ritual law) has proceeded without regard to the perfection of the individual and without regard for the centrality of ethics. This tendency has been present in every age of the Jewish people: from the biblical prophets, railing against the legalistic belief that rote sacrifices devoid of proper ethical devotion could move God, to the talmudic dictum that one must strive to do more than the law requires in interpersonal situations; from the eleventh-century moralist Baḥya ibn Pekuda, whose treatise *The Duties of the Heart* tried to correct the wrong impression that Judaism required only the fulfillment of ritual duties, to the eighteenth-century moralist Moshe Ḥayyim Luzzatto, whose *Paths of the Upright* served to correct this same impression in his day; from Rav Yisrael Salanter of Lithuania, who founded an impassioned movement of like-minded scholars in order to restore the balance between ethics and ritual, to Emmanuel Levinas, the philosopher/talmudist whose philosophy critiques not only the Jewish tendency to forget the primacy of ethics but also the entire tradition of Western philosophy for having made the same mistake—the biblical commingling of purpose and means for achieving it has required frequent reiteration through the ages. Traditionally, the literature of reiteration produced is called Mussar.

In the case of Emmanuel Levinas, the project to reconnect purpose and method became all the more critical in the light of the utter failure of ethical action in the world that was the Holocaust. Since ignoring the Holocaust would have been an obscenity, both philosophy and religion—both Western culture and Jewish culture—required a radical regrounding at that juncture. However, such a confrontation does not imply the automatic rejection of everything that preceded the Holocaust. On the contrary, it may be that what preceded the Holocaust, shorn of missteps and mistakes, could be the only thing able to rescue us from the world the Holocaust has bequeathed us.

This original genius of the Hebrew Scriptures, this combination of law and ethical perfection that epitomizes the phrase "image of God," was cast anew as the focus of one of the most remarkable phenomena in Jewish experience: the emergence of the Mussar movement. It is a fascinating example of this recrudescent tendency to reiterate ethics as the goal of the study and observance of the law. It is both interesting and important to understand that this reiteration has been a continuous element of Jewish experience. This fact accounts for the presence in Jewish literature of the many ethical/pietistic treatises that became the material out of which Rav Salanter began to build his movement. The study of these oft-neglected texts was a central characteristic of his Mussar system. But just as important as the texts themselves were the new methods and supporting context that Salanter proposed for their study.

◻ ◻ ◻

We began our inquiry with a series of questions. These questions are the very questions that Mussar addresses: Why it is so difficult to do what is good? What is the relationship between living a religious life and an ethical one? How can religion fortify an ethical life? To these questions we will add one more: In a cultural milieu in which personal satisfaction and spiritual satisfaction are deemed synonymous, can we hope to attain an alternate spirituality that promises to take us beyond ourselves not through intoxication, but through profound concern for the other people among whom we live?

Through Mussar theory we will begin to answer the first questions. There is a reason why it is so difficult to do what is good, and when we know the reason there are proven strategies we can use to work toward overcoming it. There is a relationship between ethical life, which we will refer to as *middot,* and religious life, which we will refer to by the classical Jewish term *mitzvot.* Learning about that relationship will have a positive impact on us, wherever we find ourselves on the spectrum of Jewish observance—indeed, it may become a determining factor in that observance. And there is an alternate spirituality that moves us off the center of the universe, making room first of all for other people and, in the end, the Most Other as well.

To do this, we will ask more practical questions, once we have dealt with the theoretical issues. What might a contemporary Mussar practice look like? How can it be made accessible to otherwise busy and committed people? How much time does it take? Is it a spiritual practice that one embarks on alone or in groups? How are such groups formed? What are the specific ways in which *mitzvot* and *middot* interact?

Our first task will be to explain more fully the answers I found to the theological questions. Our next task will be to look more closely at the theory of Mussar as it emerges from classical Mussar texts. Our last task will be to propose a way of living in spiritual discipline, powerfully cognizant of our responsibilities to others and transformed in the process of meeting these responsibilities. This transformation results in what Jewish tradition ultimately means by holiness. Properly understood, we propose to move the possibility of holiness to the topic of our contemporary spiritual agenda.

PART ONE

Building a
Contemporary
Mussar Theology

Introduction

What Is Theology?

Theology is about making sense of the world in a way that recognizes God's involvement in the world and in our lives. Thus, to engage in theology is already to take the question of God seriously, though not necessarily to decide whether God exists or what role God plays in the world. In fact, the existence of God and the role God plays in the world are, theologically speaking, two different (albeit related) questions. Theology also includes questions about the relationship between human beings and God, as well as the impact that relationship has on the ends or goals of life.

There is not just one traditional Jewish theology. Jewish thinkers throughout the centuries have struggled with the picture of God presented in Scripture, trying to reconcile the biblical depiction with their own sense of the realities of the world. Although this process has frequently led to changes in our notions of God (compared to the original biblical images), interpreters have usually taken pains to suggest that their "new" ideas of God are, nonetheless, firmly rooted in Scripture. This claim depended on a close reading of the Bible, in order to find openings within the text upon which to hang the new worldview. This process is called midrash. One might, in fact, suggest that one meaning for "midrash" is "theology."

The corpus of "theological midrash" is vast, beginning even within the Bible itself, where we often find later books of the Bible offering interpretive readings of earlier biblical texts. For example, recall the passage from Exodus 34:6–7 cited in the introduction to this volume: "Adonai, Adonai, mighty, merciful and gracious, long-suffering, and abundant in love and truth, keeping truth to thousands, forgiving iniquity and transgression and sin, but who will by no means clear the guilty, but visits the iniquity of parents upon children and children's children, upon the third and fourth generation." Much later in the Bible, in the Book of Jonah, we find a very similar list: "For I know You are a compassionate and gracious God, slow to anger, abounding in kindness, renouncing punishment." Now, it is highly unlikely that the author of Jonah was unaware of the Book of Exodus and it is reasonable to presume that the list of God's qualities that he puts into Jonah's mouth differs purposely from the list in Exodus. Clearly, the author of Jonah was less comfortable, theologically, with a God who punished sinners, let alone with a God who punished the descendants of sinners for three or four generations. The author of Jonah is doing midrash on the Book of Exodus: he changes the text to bring it into conformity with his own understanding of reality (in this case: the belief in a compassionate, rather than vindictive, deity).

Historical catastrophes have often provided the impetus for a midrashic reading of Scripture. After the destruction of the First Temple in Jerusalem (sixth century B.C.E.), the prophets Jeremiah and Ezekiel responded by trying to explain to the people of Israel the reason for their suffering. Similarly, after the destruction of the

Second Temple (first century C.E.) the classical Rabbis struggled to refine their understanding of God and the relationship between God and Israel to account for the tragedies they experienced. Major shifts in theology have been reflected in new midrashic understandings of Scripture and tradition throughout Jewish history, usually in response to particular historical events. It is no surprise then that theological questions have likewise come to the fore in the aftermath of at least three major dislocations that characterize the modern Jewish experience. Firstly, the Enlightenment and the growing importance of science (as well as the related cultural concepts of individuality, diversity, and equality) required a new way of envisioning the world theologically. Secondly, the impact of mass migration and immigration that accompanied the beginning of the twentieth century thrust Jews out of what had become ancient homelands (despite their oppressiveness), into a variety of new homelands—including, but not limited to, the State of Israel. And, finally, we have the event of the Holocaust. The challenges to traditional theology presented by the first two events pale in comparison to the challenge presented by the third.

The theology presented in the following chapters has been influenced by all three of these events. It assumes that our theological language must be clarified. We need to know how, in the light of these realities, we can continue to use traditional theological terms, and we also need to know how to relate to Scripture and other traditional texts. Additionally, we must use language that we find compelling, which will allow us to make sense of our world and to find a place within that sense for God. In order for this to claim to be a Jewish theology it must be compatible with the Torah and the interpretive tradition that it gave rise to, and it must use the same primary theological terms that the tradition has used throughout generations for theological discourse.

One of the clearest ways to address the full range of theological subjects is under the traditional rubrics of creation, revelation, and redemption. These terms describe the three main questions that must be addressed in order for any theology to be compelling: Where do we come from? What must we do? And where are we going? Those indeed are the questions of the hour, just as they have been the questions of the ages.

CHAPTER ONE

Creation

To study creation is to address the question: Where do we
come from? We do not mean by this question to ask about
the physical forces that bring us into existence. Questions of
that sort are rightly left to the pursuit of science. Recognizing that
science's ability to address such questions is of relatively recent vin-
tage, it is understandable that ancient scriptural accounts of creation
would mix three legitimate human pursuits together—namely, theology, philosophy, and science. Whereas theology is about making sense
of the world in a way that recognizes God's involvement, philosophy
is about making sense of the world only according to the canons of
reason. In this sense theology and philosophy are distinct disciplines,
while science was born of philosophy. In recent centuries, however,
science and philosophy have also distinguished themselves from each
other: science applies reason solely to the data of the natural world,
while philosophy applies reason to the metaphysical world (e.g., by
asking questions such as "What is our purpose?" or "Why are we
here?"). Over the last 100 to 150 years, philosophy has been unable
to answer these questions as long as it insists that only reason, and not

God, can enter into the equation. Despite this emerging distinction between philosophy and science, philosophy remains nevertheless wedded to the same principles as science and the ancient question remains no less compelling: What forces bring us to know the difference between right and wrong—in other words, what is the origin of moral life? The question thus posed has enormous implications for behavioral and ethical concerns, making creation an appropriate starting-point in crafting a theology for Mussar.

We will begin by looking briefly at some of the salient verses from the Torah that describe creation, from the two complementary stories that the Torah uses to address this subject:

> When God began to create heaven and earth—the earth being unformed and void, with darkness over the surface of the deep and a wind from God sweeping over the water—God said, "Let there be light," and there was light. God saw that the light was good . . . (Genesis 1:1–4, JPS)

God would declare parts of the creation "good" five more times before calling the whole of it "very good." This first description of creation declares in no uncertain terms that creation is good and that it is a gift to humans. The world comes into existence before any human consciousness and is there to nurture that consciousness.

In the second description of creation we read a more complex story. In it the world also exists before human beings, but this story seems almost uninterested in the details of this pre-existence. Instead, it focuses on the creation of the human being and dwells on the loneliness implicit in being human without relation. The first human being is instructed to choose between good and evil (which, in later chapters, I will call the very meaning of human consciousness). This human being, who owes obedience to his Creator, is immediately given a clear commandment. And, as opposed to what is good, we learn what is not good: "It is not good for man to be alone" (Genesis 2:18).

Thus by posing the question "Where do we come from?" the Torah begins to provide the outline of an answer. The words themselves, *bereshit bara* ("when God began to create"), proclaim that we do not bring ourselves into moral life. Rather, another brings us into consciousness of ourselves, which then entails certain debts and responsibilities to the other. In other words, we develop a sense of moral obligation as a result of the care of another. The memory of this care becomes an ideal, a place where we are able to return for solace throughout our lives. When something occurs in the course of our life that precipitates our search for this solace, this return to origins, we can say that we are engaged in a spiritual search.

When we seek the solace of the spirit, we seek a return to what we have known concretely and intimately from our experience in the world: pleasure. We have, from infancy, been drawn into the world by the pleasure we receive: the physical nurture, the touch of another person, and the responsiveness of others to our needs. Even though pleasure may not always be our predominant sensation, its effect is so powerful that our memory of pleasure never fades. We learn to cultivate pleasure under the most difficult circumstances. Enjoyment of pleasure persists as a significant motivation at each moment of our lives.

My theology about creation thus begins with the recognition that pleasure is at the core of what it means to be human. Others might begin by wondering why we exist at all, or by asking whether anything in the world exists outside of our own minds. (These have been the classic questions of philosophy and religion expressed as ontology and epistemology.) Others might also ponder the reality of physical pain, or our need for shelter, warmth, and food—and argue that it is these needs that make the real life of the spirit worth seeking. Thus they might counsel us to suppress our physical needs in order to avoid the seduction of enjoyment; this is the ascetic impulse in religious tradition. In so doing, however, they deny the simple facts of our human existence: in our everyday life we seek enjoyment, we seek to fulfill our needs—both physical and emotional—because it feels good.

This notion of goodness is affirmed in the familiar biblical narrative of creation in which God is depicted as deriving satisfaction from creation, declaring it "good" and "very good" (*tov* and *tov me'od,* in Genesis 1). Both the story and our real-life experience teach that the pursuit of pleasure and the experience of pleasure (i.e., enjoyment) are sources of the good. Experiencing this goodness establishes the filter through which all other questions are framed. Seeking and enjoying pleasure prove incontrovertibly that the world outside of us is real. We become the people we are through pleasure, through reaching out into the real world. The incontrovertible experience of enjoying the external world also provides at least an interim answer to the other philosophic question we cited above: "Why do we exist rather than not?" This might be answered by suggesting simply that the goal of existence is enjoyment. Certainly the biblical story, with its emphasis on God's satisfaction with creation, would suggest that this is indeed the answer. We exist in order to enjoy the good that is implicit in enjoying the world outside of ourselves.

This enjoyment of pleasure also creates in us a sense of gratitude, a debt we owe the other who is the source of our pleasure. The biblical story in Genesis 2 also mirrors this sense of obligation in the command by God to human beings to tend the Garden. The good that we seek, the solace that returns us to a sense of that good despite its distance from us, persists unrelentingly. We must continuously fill our needs: of warming ourselves and feeding ourselves and clothing ourselves. We never tire of receiving emotional support, the comfort and caressing that brings some small pleasure even amidst pain. Argument can never convince us to desist from this quest: as long as we persist in life we persist in the pursuit of pleasure. Certainly, we may sometimes be convinced by various arguments to abandon or even condemn this pursuit, but this abandonment sets up in our psyches an explosive tension, sometimes even transforming the rejection of enjoyment into a new understanding of what is enjoyable for us. But in most cases we are beset with a pain worse than any physical pain when enjoyment is spurned. This is the way of the world and the way of the human beings in the world, and it is so basic to our constitution that we have placed it at the very beginning of our story describing the creation of the world.

The theology that I have constructed embraces the enjoyment of pleasure as the core experience of being human. We do not deny our experience of the world, but rather cherish it; in doing so we marvel at the power that this force has in our lives. We identify enjoyment of pleasure as the force of life itself. We persist; we seek this enjoyment. Deprived of enjoyment, we pine for it. Our search for the solace of the spirit is rooted in our memories of this enjoyment. We are always in search to fulfill our needs. And since that search is all we know of the world and all we remember of our consciousness as human beings, we acknowledge that the enjoyment of pleasure is not only part of us, but the very engine of our existence, the essence of our very spirit, spirit itself.

The stories of creation are then the stories of our experience of the enjoyment of pleasure and the moral implications of this experience. They teach or remind us that the search for the enjoyment of pleasure is relational—that is, pleasure is something we experience by the grace of another. The creation story further teaches or reminds us that this experience of pleasure is bound up, from our very beginnings as human beings, with that which is good. Thus as our search for pleasure develops and matures, it will increasingly recognize not only its dependence on our relationship with another, but also the conflation of pleasure and goodness. This conflation, seen in the context of being in relationship with another, gives rise to another idea that emerges theologically from the very notion of creation: love. Creation is a description of the love that is at the center of our coming into moral life, and this love grounds all of our thoughts and actions undertaken in our lives as humans.

Love is that internal emotional state achieved when fulfilling our needs leads to the pursuit of pleasure. To say that love is a complex phenomenon is an understatement. It communicates both desire for and service to another, and we will express these two aspects of love as *yirat hashem* (fear of God) and *ahavat hashem* (love of God) in later chapters. For our present purposes we recognize that love is an internal sensation, but one that is inextricably connected to something outside ourselves. We feel love when we take in or internalize enjoyment, but our love is also directed toward the source of that pleasure. Love describes the experience we have of belonging in the world and at the same time being beholden to the world and to other people in it. The pursuit of our own enjoyment would be impossible as a solitary activity, without stimulation beyond ourselves. Love is both a feeling and an acknowledgement. It ends up within us, but comes to us from the outside. We are affirmed by it, but we are indebted because of it—or, at least, we are conscious of its bi-directionality.

This bi-directional relationship that we call love is not, at first, a relationship of equality. In infancy our needs are filled exclusively from sources outside of us. We are the recipients of the enjoyment of love before we are able to direct love outward from ourselves to another. We are the recipients of the love relationship before we are its purveyors. Someone else accepts the responsibility of loving us, and this is no small responsibility. As infants, we can give back very little in tangible terms. Yet, apparently, what we can give back not only suffices but also continually increases the love that we receive. Someone else has chosen to suspend their own need to seek pleasure, and instead devote energy to giving us pleasure. Thus we must look at the other side of the love relationship as well as our own. Put another way, young children must eventually grow up and begin to reciprocate love to others, in addition to just receiving it.

In the process of growing up we continue to take the gifts offered to us, continue to seek our own pleasure, in order to shape a world for ourselves in which we belong, in which we are at home. Being "at home" comes to define our very notion of what we want for ourselves—essentially, always. As we grow into adulthood, seeking a way "home" will provide solace when we encounter difficulties in our life in the world. However, as much as being at home is comfortable and gives us pleasure, it also limits our pleasure in ways that we eventually cannot abide. Remaining "at home" maintains a world of safety that would deny a paradoxical part of our nature—that is, that we also seek to enjoy that which may not be safe. Buttressed by the comforts of home, we eventually must seek to test the world outside its walls in search of an enjoyment that comes not before disappointment but after it. In other words, even if we must risk failure in the pursuit of love, we take that risk. We are willing, even anxious, to expand the scope of pleasure available to us, by introducing to our pursuit of pleasure the possibility of failure, of pain. Despite its safety, we do leave home.

As we grow up, we soon learn that having our own needs met requires, in turn, meeting the needs of others, of another. This other evokes in us a desire not to satisfy ourselves first and foremost, but to achieve our own satisfaction through giving to this other, through fulfilling their needs in a way that satisfies them. The more the other person enjoys what we can give, the more pleasure we then experience. Our experience of love changes and deepens, insofar as we experience it now not only as its recipient but also as its giver, its source. The passivity with which we absorbed love as infants has been transformed into an activity. In this mode, love carries with it an insistence—an insistence that preoccupies us for the better part of our lives. Love insists that we remain out in the world, seeking to fulfill the needs of another and provide them with satisfaction—which is now also the way we can satisfy our own needs. The other's needs weigh upon us with a force we could not have imagined. It requires our strongest efforts, impelling us to struggle with nature itself in order to successfully satisfy this new, two-fold need. The pursuit of enjoyment populates and drives the world itself. Thus it is fitting to call this pursuit creation. We create ourselves as mature human beings and are led, in turn, to procreate, which is held to be the first *mitzvah* (commandment) in the Genesis stories.

CHAPTER TWO

Revelation

A theology of revelation addresses the question: How do we know what we must do? As we saw with creation, our use of language is telling, since using the term "revelation" already begins to point to a particular answer. The very word "revelation" proclaims that recognition of our responsibilities in the world comes to us, was revealed to us, from another source, from outside ourselves. Our understanding of creation can bring us to a certain level of self-understanding—namely, that our pursuit of pleasure cannot be limited to a passive acceptance of another's concern, but must progress to seeking the good of another. Revelation carries this concern one step further, and requires that we seek the knowledge of what that other wants. In the language of Scripture, we must love our neighbor as we love ourselves (Leviticus 19:18).

Love, once evoked, creates in us the desire to care—and this desire cannot in good conscience be abandoned. The feeling of love thus becomes transformed into a responsibility, a command to which we *must* respond. The other person who is the object of our love, and whose pleasure we seek to fulfill, now stands in a commanding position above us. The needs of someone outside of us must now be met *by us*. This love we have for another has singled us out: we are aware that no one else can stand in for us, no one else can take the responsibility off of us. We are as if elected for a particular responsibility, for a particular set of commitments. Revelation is the acknowledgment of this election.

Once we have been elected by love we are no longer independent; we have become responsible. I now experience this good as coming from somewhere outside my own being, its satisfaction entirely dependent on my relationship to another. This other, as we've seen, stands in a particular relationship to me: above and commanding. It is not a part of myself and I cannot insist that it serve my needs. On the contrary, its needs have become my own needs because I derive enjoyment in their fulfillment. In fact, I now know that this pleasure is precisely what I have been seeking all the time, and I therefore now have a deeper understanding of what I mean when I call myself an "I." I now realize that as a human being, as an individual, I am driven by my desire to satisfy another person's needs. Since there is no limit to the pleasure I desire, there is likewise no limit to the responsibility I bear to satisfy the needs of this other person. When I speak of myself in this way, when I locate in words or in thought a concept of "who I am" in this complex relationship, I am invoking the idea of what we call the soul. Revelation, the knowledge of our responsibilities in the world, is the process of acquiring— or, one might say, of constructing out of a mere self—a soul.

When it comes to our responsibilities in the world, the biblical injunction "You shall love your neighbor as yourself" is central in the classical Mussar of Rav Simḥa Zissel Braude of Kelm. This crucially important "love of neighbor" is, for Rav Simḥa, a synonym for bearing another person's burden with them. Thus love is not simply a nebulous emotion, but is rather grounded in concrete action. He writes in the first chapter of *Ḥokhmah U-Mussar:*

To reach the level of being one who bears the burden of one's fellow is impossible unless one has accustomed himself to love one's neighbor in thought and deed. . . . However, whereas the deeds of most people are observable, their thoughts are not. In order to ascertain that one loves one's neighbor in both deed and thought two criteria must be used. First we must examine the consequences of deeds and thoughts both, to be sure that they are politically constructive, for it is the political structure that sustains the world and, conversely, can shatter it. This is the lesson we learn from the destruction of the Temple, which was destroyed on account of unbridled social enmity. Since the Temple was the knot holding the world together, maintained by the treasured people, when they sinned it was erased and immediately the Temple shattered in this world. May the Exalted One return it to us speedily!

Rav Simḥa claims that the love of one's fellow human being is, in fact, the defining quality equal to bearing the burden of one's fellow. Moreover, he teaches that we cannot judge love of one's neighbors by acts alone, though judging acts is obviously easier than judging thoughts. To ascertain the quality of love one has for others, we must judge thoughts also. Finally, he teaches in no uncertain terms that the criteria by which both thoughts and acts of love are judged is social, in the sense that an act has ramifications beyond the self; our living in this world is thus infused with a sense of responsibility to others. Rav Simḥa learns this from the traditional explanation for the destruction of the Temple—namely, enmity in the social weal—and he draws out from this social idea certain implications for spiritual life. The Temple was the knot that united the material and the spiritual. Social enmity caused the erasure or untying of this knot.

Recall that in chapter 1 we suggested that there are several types of questions we might ask regarding our place in the world. Some people might first ask questions about why we exist at all, about whether the world is anything more than an extension of our own thought. Others might begin their philosophical inquiry by inquiring about our physicality, the pains and privations of the flesh to which we are prone. However, I believe that the most compelling place to begin constructing a theology is by accepting the quest for pleasure as the orienting point of all human experience (and this approach will provide a basis from which to address the other philosophical questions as well).

The first question, about existence or being, is misleading because it is too limited in its scope. It isolates the individual and wonders why just *this* particular individual exists. But we have seen, rather, that each individual comes into being in the context of loving relationships, which effectively establish satisfaction, pleasure, or goodness. Our experience suggests that we are unique because once someone else rivets our attention, we cannot escape our responsibility to that person. Thus that person and I exist together and for the sole purpose of serving one another. But this service, or love, is a complicated matter, since we can be either the subject of love (in which case we are obligated or elected), or the object of love (in which case we are served by another, who is obligated to us). Our existence is relational, and we may fluctuate within our relationships, sometimes as subject and sometimes as object. The real world is simply too complex and too fluid to be addressed adequately by the static question about existence. To reframe the question, we must ask not how an individual is precipitated into being, but rather how a soul is formed. This change in language is critical and is meant to indicate the range of experiences we have considered. A "being," an anonymous individual, may be problematic for our thought, but a "soul" describes a prior relationship, which only later calls into being an "I." "Being" in that sense is not the first question. Rather, the first question must be: To whom are we responsible, and for whom are we responsible, such that we become individuals? In philosophic terms this means we place ethics before being (or ontology) and come to a picture of being that follows ethics and is explained by it.

The second question that might be asked is about the distinction between what is real and what we think. However, this question is too limited as well. To the extent that we think at all, we think first of our pleasure, of satisfying our most basic needs. Without such satisfaction we simply would not think at all. Thus to the extent that we think, it is because someone else has met our needs. At the very least, then, something or someone outside of us must be real enough to nurture us—establishing that thought (i.e., reason), like being, *follows* ethics (i.e., the complex web of interpersonal relationships). Without nurture, without love and its responsibilities, thought could not develop.

So, it is to the third question raised earlier that we must turn. This is the question of our physicality, the question of the pleasure that we seek to attain. We must ask first whether the fact of our physicality can be consistent with our claim that love derives from pleasure. If it cannot, then we must ask: What purpose, in a world shaped by love, do the privations of the flesh serve? Or, put another way: What is the relationship of physical life to suffering, and what possible purpose can suffering serve in such a world? This question looms large in constructing our theology. We have established how the soul comes to be. Now we must ask how the soul is safeguarded and why it must be so.

Safeguarding the Soul

We begin this inquiry by returning to the distinction we've made between the two perspectives present in the experience of love, since this distinction is crucial for understanding the experience of suffering. When we, as individuals, are the objects (or recipients) of love, suffering is always unjustified, meaningless, and useless. We are served only by that which serves our own good, that which gives us pleasure, and that which we enjoy—and pain, suffering, trauma, and tragedy do not do that.

When we are the object of love, our own suffering is useless. However, when we are the subjects of love, the providers of love, the suffering of the object of our love is not useless. Their suffering devastates us, filling our consciousness and compelling us to act, oblivious to our own needs, on their behalf. The suffering of my beloved commands me to act on their behalf. The source of my good is the alleviation of my beloved's suffering.

Suffering can only be justified from the subjective perspective—that is, suffering seems to serve a purpose only when we find ourselves in the role of the nurturer, the one who meets the needs of another. From the perspective of the one who receives love, suffering cannot be justified; indeed, the very attempt to do so can itself inflict even greater suffering. Those who would suggest to me that my pain is for my own good effectively deny my defining experience, deny the constituting energy of my own person. But those who are attentive to my suffering, those who would be devastated by it and consequently act on my behalf to relieve it, succeed in rendering my suffering meaningful—for them, but never for me. When they succeed in alleviating my pain, when my suffering is assuaged, then I will certainly feel good. I will also feel grateful to them, for their love and for their obedience to the commandment of my suffering. But this will never make me grateful for the pain I have suffered.

Acting under the command of my beloved's suffering, I am in danger of surrendering myself too completely to that command. The point of seeking out the love of another and responding to that command is precisely not to surrender myself, but rather to discover the parameters of the other. To lose myself in the process would be to abandon the responsibility that I have taken on for the other. To abandon that responsibility would return my very being to the anonymity of pre-existence, out of which my soul has been formed by the love of another for me and has been enriched by my love for the other. Love creates us, but can endanger our survival. Parameters must be established to prevent this from happening.

The Emergence of Law *(Halakhah)*

In order for us not to lose ourselves in this way, the command of the other must be tempered; this happens by the creation of law. Law establishes guidelines to help us balance our desire to respond to the needs of another person, on the one hand, and our equivalent need to respond to ourselves, on the other hand. Law is the human, reasoned solution to an infinite demand, which cannot be fully met by a finite creature, by human beings. The wisdom of the law, infused by this infinite demand, reflects the partnership between infinite demand and the limited reason of human intelligence. Law is always imperfect, but seeks to inspire the possibility of perfection invoked by the unreachable infinite demand. The human reaction to the infinite demand is embodied in a commitment to justice, but it strives to go beyond justice, seeking to attain a horizon of perfection, what we may call the messianic possibility. The subject of messianism takes us from the theological category of revelation to that of redemption, to which we will return in the next chapter.

The soul is always torn between the commands of the law and other commands, which are more demanding than the law—namely, the responsibilities of meeting the needs of another, called into existence out of our love for that other. This creates tension between surrender of the self, on the one hand, and loyalty to the law shorn of its infinite command, on the other. To maintain the balance between these two competing demands is the role of religion properly understood—and of Judaism in particular. This is why Judaism understands revelation in terms of law. In order to maintain a consciousness of the demanding nature of this balance, the Mussar movement created a pedagogy intended to navigate this chasm. Mussar is loyal to the law, but vigilantly awake to the demands of the command beyond the law.

There are other threats to the soul besides the threat of surrender. If it is true that loving another person can dissolve one's own sense of self, then it is also true that being the object of another's love can do the same. That is because when we focus exclusively on being the object of another's love, it allows us to avoid the responsibilities of ourselves becoming lovers—which is the more mature, more difficult role to take on. This is not only a problem in human relationships, but can occur in the religious context as well. When individuals aspire to become the object of God's love and nothing more, they avoid the responsibilities of human love. It is possible to become intoxicated by the dream of being enveloped by divine love, and hence to imagine that God is the only worthy object of one's love. Since our most primal love emerges from our interactions with other people, it is merely wishful thinking—dreaming if you will—that allows us to bypass those people for a so-called direct experience of God's love. In this dreaming the true soul is threatened with annihilation.

Finally we come to the nature of the threat to the soul—regardless of how that threat originates (that is, whether from our self-abnegation in the face of an all-consuming responsibility to another; or whether from a failure to respond to another because of an exclusive focus on having our own needs met). The ultimate threat to the soul is sleep. Once the other has called us, once we have fallen in love, we are enjoined to a life of never-ending responsibility. This love has taken away from us the ever-present luxury of infancy: the freedom to fall asleep at will. As adults, we must always be wakeful and on guard; we must sleep with one eye open, as parents learn to do in the presence of their children. Yet to live in a state of such sleeplessness is exhausting. We seek relief, which can come at the hands of yet others for whom we have not yet accounted. We do not live in the world alone with our beloved. We live in a broader community. We do so, in large part, so that the demands of infinite commandment, the demand of sleeplessness, can be shared. We develop institutions that serve as buffers and refuges for us in our exhaustion. Without such a community the sleeplessness required by love would be unbearable. Community helps us to bear the infinite responsibility for the other that we must not shirk. We look to our community's institutions to help us negotiate the tension between taking on all of our own responsibilities all the time, single-handedly, and ceding to the community all of those responsibilities. Standing somewhere between the infinite demand of the other and our desire to sleep the sleep of infants are our relationships with family, friends, congregation, civic organization, and even the organs of state. There will always be those who are prepared to support the community fully as long as they are relieved of their own infinite responsibility, as well as those who will reject the community in favor of near-mad sleeplessness. It is the work of religion—and very much so the goal of the Mussar movement in Judaism—to create a balance between these two poles. How are we to cede to the community some of our responsibility for one another, without losing sight of the fact that those responsibilities are ultimately our own, as individuals?

As we have seen, the soul is threatened on the one hand by surrender and on the other by sleep. Law and social structures function to protect the soul against the first of these threats. For the second, a discipline that promises to keep the care of the other always in our vision is needed. Our spiritual search is intimately tied to the well-being of those whom we love. Our care and our obligation to care extend far beyond the circle of our closest family and friends (although it must always begin there and return there) to include, at the extreme, the entirety of humanity. This is our spiritual quest, unencumbered by dreams or by sleep or by surrender. If we are determined not to miss the opportunity, we must cultivate wakefulness. Yet how do we do so and still avoid the madness that such wakefulness can bring on? It is to this question that we now turn our attention. But first, we need to explore the contours of this wakefulness a bit more closely.

We have shown that although enjoyment is the driving force of our existence, it is a complex enjoyment that is dependent on our ability to satisfy the needs of others. This desire to satisfy the needs of another literally becomes the main factor in defining what we mean when we call ourselves human beings. What we mean by the "ego" is now understood as including not only the satisfaction of our own needs as the recipients of love, but also our desires as the givers of love, as lovers of others. Rabbi Akiva believed that the central principle of Judaism was encapsulated in Leviticus 19:18, "You shall love your neighbor as yourself." In the following Mussar text, the view of Rabbi Akiva is accepted as binding. In the light of our discussion to this point, we can understand what Rabbi Akiva is saying: to love one's neighbor is to love oneself. There is no self to love, in the end, unless that self has developed beyond mere self-love (or beyond a willingness to be loved by others), and has truly become a self by virtue of loving others (one's "neighbor," in the language of the text).

Rav Simḥa Zissel found this statement of Rabbi Akiva equally compelling. He writes in *Ḥokhmah U-Mussar:*

> We have already introduced the idea that a person's cleaving to the spiritual Torah is impossible unless that person has become a person of spirit

—this is one in whom there is a true unified soul. Our Sages well understood that "To love your neighbor as yourself, this is the great principle of the Torah" (Genesis Rabbah 24:8). For a person of spirit, the master of a fine soul, the soul is attached to the Torah through love, through observance in thought and deed. Such a love enables the crude materiality of one's nature to undergo a thorough spiritual cleansing.

Rav Simha here explains that the biblical verse "Love your neighbor as yourself" is precisely about "bearing the burden of the other"—and that this is indeed *the* "great principle" of the Torah. For Rav Simha, there would be no Torah were it not for this love, which is the bearing of the burden of the other. The Torah would, as it were, remain unattached to the human soul. It might exist but its existence would be hidden, meaningless from the human perspective. At the same time, without this love, which is the bearing of the burden of the other, there would also be no true human being. What we can rightfully call a human being is precisely that mode of existence effected by bearing another's burden. This love purifies the soul. It makes the human a "master of a fine soul," that is, one who has attained mastery over the self's physical needs and is therefore able to give oneself up to become attached to Torah, to and through love of another. Yet, this love comes to us as a command, an imperative: "Love your neighbor as yourself!" It comes from outside the self and, revealing itself as our obligation, it creates us as human beings. We, who are masters of the fine soul, submit to the command. This Rav Simha calls spiritual cleansing.

One of the questions, then, that we must ask ourselves is: Who is our neighbor? The answer to this question is never definitive, but rather evolving. The word for "neighbor" in Hebrew, *re'a,* is derived from the same root as the word for "pasturing" or "shepherding." The definition of "my neighbor" thus might be: the person for whom I am responsible. The question becomes, of course: Who is the person for whom I am responsible? However, if we have an insatiable desire (re'ut, in Hebrew) to meet the needs of those for whom we are responsible, and this becomes the very intentionality of our consciousness (that is, the structure of our thought [ra'ayon in Hebrew]), then the answer to our question must be that our "neighbor" is a constantly expanding category. The one who is closest to us, literally our beloved, is our first neighbor. But the very experience of such a responsibility itself increases our need for such responsibility, driving the list outward to include family, friends, ethnic and national affinities, and, ideally, ultimately all of humanity and all of creation. And then where are we? This insatiable desire may indeed be seen as an infinite desire, and the satisfaction of such an infinite desire is only possible by an "infinite beloved." These terms, although inadequate, are not meaningless. By analyzing our mundane human characteristics, we are able to reach a place where we can use terms that meaningfully go beyond or transcend our human dimension. To speak of an Infinite Beloved is to be able to speak of God.

To speak of this God is to speak of an experience that we can imagine but that is always in our future. To speak of this God is to speak of an experience that is forever receding beyond the terms of our relationships with people. To speak of this God is to speak of that possibility of coming home that we earlier described as the end of a never-ending journey. Our language is challenged to its limits, yet the idea still makes sense. The burden that we assume first for our nearest beloved is only an intimation of the burden that we must ultimately assume for our Infinite Beloved. These two burdens are not simply analogous, but are rather points along the same path. And since the Infinite Beloved is infinite not only in what we might imagine as a "going forward" direction, but also in a "going backward" direction, then we bear the infinite burden of our Infinite Beloved as much as what we perceive to be the beginning of our journey as we do at what we perceive to be its end.

The Infinite Beloved and our infinite burden for our Beloved are as equally present in our first act of love as they are in our last. Without that burden, what are we?

The Spirit we seek and the solace that we desire are not easy to achieve, but rather seem to be a burden. Only by embracing that burden—rather than avoiding it—can we cultivate our souls and prepare them for the encounter we ultimately desire. We cannot attain the solace at the end of the journey if we bypass the journey itself. Bypassing the journey leads to disappointment, which pains us. Disappointment does not give us pleasure and we go to sleep in order to hide from the pain, to seek some sort of pleasure wherever we can. Sleep is the great pain reliever. But as long as we are alive, we will always eventually awaken—and when we do, our disappointments will only have multiplied. We must understand that it is not in our best interests to sleep; on the contrary, it is in our best interests to stay more awake than we've ever been. It is in our best interests to re-experience the pleasure that comes from caring for another. To seek the care of another is the spiritual path of Mussar.

When we bear the responsibility for another, we also awaken in that other person a desire. Their experience of receiving our love awakens them to their own desire to be the provider of love to yet another person. Those whom we love may not only love us back but may also love others. As they do so, the care of the soul is accomplished. As individuals nurture their own souls through care of another, sleep is less and less an option for each individual.

As we have seen, our goal is the development of the soul, not the development of the self per se. The development of the self, or the ego, must precede the development of the soul. The ego develops as the object of love, but the soul develops as love's subject. The full development of the soul is dependent on the development of a healthy ego. A lover must have been beloved. A healthy ego is transformed into a soul only via the burden of another—who must impinge on the ego, causing the ego to shrink, as it were. The beloved implicitly asks: "Why are you, if it is not to care for me?" The ego has no answer, but the soul does. The discipline of Mussar asks a great deal from the individual. It asks one to efface one's ego and to replace it, so to speak, with a soul. Mussar asserts that doing so will give the individual a sense of satisfaction, in the process of addressing his or her own desires. The desires will not be met, for that is an infinite process—but addressing the desires will fill the person with a sense of satisfaction. However, those whose own needs have not been met will find frustration, as they attempt to efface their own needs prematurely in favor of the needs of another.

A central part of Mussar education is devoted to learning how to learn to bear another's burden together with that other person, without allowing one's own needs to be neglected or overshadowed. At the heart of Rav Simḥa Zissel's Mussar is the development of what he calls "an imaginative projection." This is the ability to view the world through the needs of another. He treats the subject of this "imaginative projection" in many sections of *Ḥokhmah U-Mussar,* such as the following:

> We find in the Zohar, *Parshat Mishpatim:* "And they saw . . . a paved work of sapphire and it was as the very heaven for clearness." We have already written about this, that it requires a great deal of inner wisdom to speak on this. About that which we cannot speak, we can only write. The biblical text must be explained. "A paved work of sapphire"— Rashi explains that this means the memory of Israel's pain. Thus we see how great is the power of doing the commandments in this world—so much that when the Holy One, so to speak, uses the world of deeds for Israel, God forms an imaginative projection as if God made of the deeds a work of sapphire, to remember the pain of Israel . . .

Rav Simḥa introduces a biblical image that will illustrate how imaginative projection—the key to a Mussar way of seeing—is also the way God sees. In fact, it is by allowing humans (Moses, the

Elders of Israel) to also see this way that God became the first Mussar teacher. However, Rav Simḥa is understandably cautious. He must make this point by recourse to classical kabbalistic texts, which deal with matters about which it is impossible to speak. We are forced to speak of God in human terms and this must be done only with the knowledge that such terms are not to be taken literally.

The biblical passage under discussion reads in full: "Then Moses and Aaron, Nadab and Abihu, and seventy elders of Israel ascended; and they saw the God of Israel; under His feet there was the likeness of a pavement of sapphire, like the very heavens for purity. Yet He did not raise His hand against the leaders of the Israelites; they beheld God and they ate and drank" (Exodus 24:9–11). According to Rashi, this "pavement of sapphire" (i.e., the stonework beneath the feet of God, perhaps supporting the divine throne) is constructed of the memory of Israel's pain. The pain appears translucent: it can be seen through and the view is "the very heavens for purity" or clearness. What is important for Rav Simḥa to establish is that the world we live in, the world of deeds, constitutes the world for God. It is human activity that God "uses" in seeing the world. God, too, forms an imaginative projection from those deeds. This is the work of sapphire.

Why, Rav Simḥa asks, is this projection made up of the pain of Israel, especially since the deeds that God uses to construct the world are those performed by Israel in obedience to God's commandments, which we would think would produce joy? Rav Simḥa explores the irremissibility of this-worldly pain in a passage we will examine in chapter 3. For now, however, we cannot leave this paragraph without commenting on the biblical context for this incredible vision that Rav Simḥa is explicating—that is, the climactic point which, following tried and true rabbinic technique, Rav Simḥa does not mention explicitly but assumes that we are aware of. The crucial point is that this "seeing" of the world through the bearing of the burden of the other—a "seeing" that is definitive of both human and divine being—is followed by the act of eating and drinking. The spiritual vision is anchored in what we might call the miracle of materiality. This vision of human and divine compassion is not thought to be at the expense of flesh and blood obligations. Rather, the God who can bear the burden of creation must allow humans to eat and drink, in fact must provide the food and drink for them.

◧ ◧ ◧

Our goal in seeking the life of the spirit is to return to a pristine experience of pleasure. It is through the idea of revelation that we have explored the source and extent of our obligations for another. To this goal we have added the demands that these obligations make on us. That turns our attention from means to ends. Both creation and revelation, therefore, naturally draw our attention toward the third question we set out to answer by engaging in theology: Where are we going? This is the question that is considered under the rubric of redemption.

CHAPTER THREE

Redemption

Redemption addresses the question: Where are we going? As we saw with both creation and revelation, posing this question in this way already influences the contours of the answer. The very word "redemption" suggests that where we are is not where we ultimately want to be and that it is desirable to be somewhere else. Much ink has been spilled in an effort to physically describe the place toward which we are headed. These attempts frequently assume that "redemption" implies another world and a different definition of life. Usually this other world is not only spatially different from the world in which we live, but is also temporally different, located in another time—a time after this life, or an "afterlife." There is no denying that most religions use these terms to conceptualize and communicate these difficult concepts. However, despite the tendency to understand this future world in either spatial or temporal terms, it is not necessary to do so. Certainly within Jewish tradition, it was tacitly understood that these ideas were precisely metaphors, used to describe via spatial and temporal imagery a change in the *dimension* in which this life is experienced.

Therefore, when we speak of redemption (or the question of where are we going), we remain concerned with the phenomenon of moral life—just as we were with our understanding of the terms creation and revelation. Thus the question is: In light of the debts we owe others as a consequence of our own creation, and in light the obligations that we become aware of as a consequence of revelation, what change in our experience of the moral life can we expect? We will begin to answer this question with a continuation of Rav Simḥa's commentary of *Parshat Mishpatim*. He writes:

> And now we add to this wondrous insight (about the brickwork of sapphire). A well-known saying of the wise: "Pain and joy are interlaced with one another"—that is, after pain will come joy and the joy will be much greater than if one hadn't experienced the pain before the joy. And now: "When they saw it was as the heaven for clearness" they were already redeemed. Why did the Torah need to add the phrase "a pavement of sapphire" as a memorial to the pain of Israel? Only, it would seem, that God had before them the pavement of sapphire in contrast to the very heavens for clearness to raise, as it were, the joy in contrast to this. And obviously God, the Blessed One, has no need of this. Rather it is to teach God's love for the treasured people and to teach all humanity how important is the obligation of bearing the burden with one's fellows, to be sorry in their sorrow and to rejoice in their joy. And this is a wonder of wonders, that God helps us to understand this wondrous height.

Rav Simḥa continues to explore this divine imaginative projection in light of a "saying of the wise," reaching a "wondrous insight." The insight addresses the seeming centrality of pain in human life—even human life lived in accordance with the divine commandments.

The answer is, to begin with, that pain and joy are necessarily interlaced. Firstly, this means that all pleasure includes an element of pain, insofar as the pleasure itself does not fully satisfy us. Moreover, we must recognize that pain is a precursor to pleasure. Pain is what we might call a "baseline" that allows for the experience of pleasure.

This insight leads Rav Simḥa to ask a remarkable question concerning redemption. Since Moses and the elders were brought up to see God's throne after the redemption (from Egypt), why did the Torah refer to the sapphire brickwork, which functioned as a memorial of Israel's pain? What use is pain for a people recently redeemed—who, presumably, still bear the memory of pain close at hand? It was necessary precisely because redemption was not simply the liberation from slavery, but rather must be understood as bearing of the burden of the other—which continues well beyond the physical redemption from Egypt. This idea, which Rav Simḥa calls a great height or high level of understanding, is taught to us by God. Although God has no personal need for sapphire brickwork, it girds the divine throne as an act of loving/teaching, or Mussar—so that we might understand this important lesson.

Thus, to bear the burden of the other leads to redemption and sustains redemption. It also leads to the bearing of the burden of the Other/Creator and it also invokes the Other/Creator to bear the burden of creation itself. This is a creation fashioned out of human deeds, weighed down by pain grounding even its pleasure, but a creation that can be transcended through the bearing of the burden of the other.

In order to further elaborate on the difficult notions of redemption, eternity, and the world to come, we will turn to another central text of Mussar literature: *Mesillat Yesharim,* or *The Path of the Upright,* by Rabbi Moshe Ḥayyim Luzzatto, also known as the Ramḥal. Luzzatto himself was born in Padua, Italy in 1706 into one of the most important families in Italian Jewry. Well-versed in Bible, Talmud, midrash, and halakhic literature (as well as contemporary Italian and scientific culture), he was regarded as a genius from childhood. But Luzzatto's true genius emerged in kabbalistic studies, to which he eventually attracted a group of young students. In 1727, Luzzatto claimed to hear a divine voice that he believed was sent to reveal heavenly secrets. Luzzatto was accused of participating in the same sort of messianic speculation that had destabilized Jewish communities around the world during the previous century, when great movements of Jews had followed the false messiah Shabbatai Zevi. The established Jewish community reacted swiftly and forcefully: Luzzatto was forbidden to teach Kabbalah. Feeling hounded by the authorities in Padua, he eventually made his way to Amsterdam. Here too he was forbidden to teach or write about Kabbalah, but he did produce a series of theological and ethical treatises, the most important of which was *Mesillat Yesharim*. This book, published in 1740 in Amsterdam, became an important ethical work throughout the Jewish world and was studied with particular fervor in the Mussar *yeshivot*.

Mesillat Yesharim describes a path to holiness constructed of the most essential and important character traits. The excerpts that follow deal specifically with the question of redemption, and provide a textual grounding to broaden what we have already said about this question of where we are going. In chapter 1 of *Mesillat Yesharim,* Luzzatto writes:

> The foundation of saintliness and the root of perfection in the service of God lies in a person's coming to see clearly and to recognize as a truth the nature of one's duty in the world, and the ends toward which one should direct one's vision, and the aspirations in all of one's labors throughout one's life. The Sages of blessed memory have taught us that human beings were created solely for the purpose of rejoicing in God and deriving pleasure from the splendor of God's Presence; for this is true joy and the greatest pleasure that can be found. The place where this joy may truly be derived is the world to come, which was expressly created to provide for it [the joy]. However, the path to the object of

our desire is *this* world, as our Sages of blessed memory have said: "This world is like a corridor to the world to come" (Avot 4:21).

One of the chief insights of Judaism is the recognition that joy is a driving force of human life. Joy and our pursuit of pleasure constitute the primary impulses of human behavior. Certainly the pursuit of pleasure can be corrupted, and certainly the options available to us in this pursuit require some objective standard of evaluation. These concerns, however, do not for one minute lessen the commitment that we have to the central idea that human perfection and human joy are synonymous. It is essential and remarkable to note that already in *Mesillat Yesharim* the recognition of joy as the goal of human life is underscored. This idea will become increasingly important as we continue to develop Mussar consciousness.

According to *Mesillat Yesharim,* finding this joy and defining its nature are central to the religious quest. The end of the quest is presented as being beyond the structures of the world we know, "this world." Instead, the perfection or joy is placed beyond, in the "world to come." This messianic gesture, so crucial to Ramḥal, is somewhat confusing to us. It is confusing since in contemporary religious discourse, we tend to understand such phrases within the context of a mythic structure that we reject, and so we have not developed a spiritual vocabulary in which such phrases can be used meaningfully. The essential nature of this messianic gesture will become clearer as we proceed through *Mesillat Yesharim* and develop our Mussar consciousness further. Yet we cannot ignore it here at the very beginning. At this point, it will suffice to say that since the possibility of pleasure and the experience of joy are never completely satisfied, but rather always—and, we might say, infinitely—stretch before us, the very ideas of pleasure and joy would be rendered meaningless without a term for this very endlessness. The term "world to come" functions to suggest this endlessness.

Luzzatto writes further:

> The means that lead a person to this goal [i.e., attaining joy] are the
> *mitzvot,* which we are commanded by Adonai, may God's name be
> blessed. The place of the performance of the *mitzvot* is in this world
> alone. Therefore, human beings were placed in this world first—so that
> by these means, which were provided for them here, they would be
> able to reach the place that has been prepared for them—namely, the
> world to come, there to be sated with the goodness that they acquired
> through them [the *mitzvot*]. As our Sages of blessed memory have said:
> "Today for their [the *mitzvot*] performance and tomorrow for receiving
> their reward (Eruvin 22a)."

This passage articulates two of Luzzatto's fundamental beliefs. The
first is that the goal of attaining joy is achieved through performance of the commandments. The second is that achieving this
joy—the infinite joy that can only be expressed by the term "the
world to come"—is the functional equivalent of achieving goodness, or the good. Both of these ideas are of crucial importance
throughout *Mesillat Yesharim.*

The idea that joy comes to us through the commandments is
counter-intuitive, especially for those of us who live in the post-
Enlightenment world of the West. We tend to think of "joy" in
terms of spontaneity, as a release from obligation, rather than in
terms of taking on obligations and fulfilling them. Yet, if we aspire
to create for ourselves an authentic Jewish spirituality, it is precisely
in this seemingly counter-intuitive mode that we must do so. As
we've seen above, both the notion of enjoyment and the notion of
love are fundamental to the Jewish experience. In addition, the
notion of *ḥasidut* must enter into the discussion at this point.
Related to the Hebrew word *ḥesed,* or lovingkindness, the most
appropriate translation for *ḥasidut* in our context may be "saintliness," and this characteristic cannot be understood apart from the
concept of love. A *ḥasid,* then, is a lover, and the experience of a

lover that we strive for is an experience of being encumbered. For one who truly loves, it is the commandment-like need to provide goodness for the beloved that turns love from sentiment to substance—from the realm of thought to that of action—from the self-absorption of self to true saintliness.

"Goodness" and "commandment" are then intimately connected. We first encounter goodness, as it were, through our actions on behalf of the beloved. As we continue our theological exploration, we will need to address questions such as: What are our obligations to our beloved? Who, indeed, is that beloved? What, if any, are the limits of our obligations? However, already in these first two paragraphs by Luzzatto, we have begun to explore the important ideas of pleasure and joy, which give rise to the twin concepts of command and goodness. Hovering above all of these is the idea of an excess or infinite context, which is necessary for the ideas to make sense in the world that we inhabit. This excess we have termed "the world to come."

Luzzatto continues to develop this idea of the relationship between goodness and commandment, as follows:

> When you look further into this matter, you will see that only union with God constitutes true perfection, as King David said, "But as for me, the nearness of God is my good (Psalms 73:28)," and "I asked one thing from God; that will I seek- to dwell in God's house all the days of my life . . . (Psalms 27:4)." This alone is the true good, and anything besides this that people deem good is nothing but emptiness and deceptive worthlessness. For people to attain this good it is certainly fitting that they first labor and persevere in exertions to acquire it. That is, they should persevere so as to unite themselves with the Blessed One by means of actions that result in this end. These actions are *mitzvot*.

In this complex paragraph, Ramḥal further elucidates the subtle connections between the idea of the good, the search for spiritual perfection, and the mystical unification of the human and the

Divine. We note that he does not introduce these more mystical ideas until after he has already described the human pursuit of pleasure, the quest for the good that presents itself in and through the commandments. The idea of infinity, in the form of the world to come, is introduced before Luzzatto proceeds to discuss specifically the idea of union with the Divine. Unless the notion of the infinite has entered our vocabulary, so to speak, then more specific perceptions of the Divine make no sense. It is for this reason that we, and Ramḥal, have from the beginning placed such importance on the idea of the world to come: we have been laying the groundwork that now allows us to move on to more complex ideas about the Divine.

In this paragraph, it is the search for the good that continues to build the structure of this spirituality. It is the good that David sought that the psalm translates into an equivalent of Divine Presence. It is the experience of the good and the concomitant experience of the Divine Presence that serves, as it were, as the motivation for laboring in the study of *hasidut,* or saintliness.

Luzzatto then reaches the conclusion of this discussion, finding cosmic significance in our observance of the commandments as the linchpin upon which our attainment of infinity—of the world to come—rests:

> If you look more deeply into the matter, you will see that the world was created for the use of humanity. In truth, human beings are the center of a great balance. For if they pull after the world and are drawn further from their Creator, then they are damaged and they damage the world with them. But if they rule over themselves and unite themselves with their Creator, and if they use the world only to aid themselves in the service of their Creator, then they are uplifted and the world itself is uplifted with them. For all creatures are greatly uplifted when they serve the "whole person," who is sanctified with the holiness of the Blessed One. It is as our Sages of blessed memory have said in relation to the light that the Holy One stored away for the righteous: "When

the Holy One saw the light that had been stored away for the righteous, God rejoiced, as it is said, 'The light of the righteous rejoices
(Proverbs 13:9)' (Ḥagigah 12a)."

Once again the idea of infinity enters into the equation. When
human beings obey the commandments, they can uplift not only
themselves but indeed the entire world. To where is the world
uplifted and what does it mean to uplift the world? According to
Ramḥal, when this happens nature serves the "whole person," who
in turn carries something of the holiness that is associated with
God. This holiness is drawn from the light stored for the righteous
in the world to come. Once again, we see the fluidity of this idea
of the world to come. The light of the righteous, which is the light
created on the first day of creation (before the sun and moon were
created), is usually associated with the world to come. Here that
light is accessible in and from *this* world when the whole person
acts, through the commandments, to uplift the world. Finally, the
light stored up for the righteous is another synonym for rejoicing.
The sanctity to which the whole person can bring the world
through the acceptance and fulfillment of commandments is a
great joy. The message of this passage is thus a weighty one.
Human beings are capable of feeling joy and bringing joy into the
world, but these capabilities carry with them grave responsibilities.
The world, in effect, depends on us and our actions.

Thus, the idea of redemption—in both my own theology and
in the traditional Mussar texts we've examined—is grounded in
the conviction that the world to come can, and ought, to form a
dimension of this world, of the world-we're-in. The fact that we
can describe redemption in this-worldly terms, however, should
not obscure the eschatological nature of this discussion. That is, we
are talking about a future horizon, a future that informs and
inspires our present, but not a future that can be made present. To
put it again in the terms we introduced earlier, wakefulness is a

necessary but unreachable goal. If we could each stay awake for one another, then the kind of ultimate transformation that redemption points toward would occur. This kind of constant wakefulness is, of course, beyond our reach. But we *can* experience moments of wakefulness, moments of great joy, and moments of weighty and encumbered love. Thus although we can talk about redemption, it must remain ahead of us and beyond our reach. It gives substance to the future and, in so doing, it is the glory of the future.

PART TWO

The Theory
of Mussar

CHAPTER FOUR

Yetzer Ha-Tov and *Yetzer Ha-Ra*

In order to practice Mussar, we must have a basic understanding of the theory upon which the practice is based. Mussar
theory is not the same as theology, although the theological
groundwork that we have laid out in previous chapters will play a
role in our discussion of Mussar theory. Mussar theory addresses
different questions than theology does. Rather than where we are
coming from or where we are going, we are now more interested
in what constitutes human consciousness in regard to the choice
between good and evil. Thus, we may consider Mussar theory to
be a special type of anthropology, a description of how and why
humans behave the ways they do.

Two terms crucial for understanding Mussar theory are *yetzer
ha-tov* and *yetzer ha-ra,* the impulse for good and the impulse for
evil. These terms are used commonly in rabbinic literature to
describe the ethical nature of human beings. According to the Talmud, each of us is created with both a *yetzer ha-tov* and a *yetzer ha-ra*
—that is, with both an urge to do good and an urge to do evil.

However, these urges are not equally matched. Left to our own devices we would choose the *yetzer ha-ra* every time over the *yetzer ha-tov.* It is for this reason that we need the guidance of the Torah.

It is important to note that both of these impulses are considered normative and necessary for human life. While the Rabbis were quick to point out that there would be no compassion in the world without the *yetzer ha-tov,* they were just as quick to point out that were it not for the *yetzer ha-ra* the world would come to an end—that is, the greed and lust that lie behind our sexual and acquisitive drives are necessary for us to procreate and acquire the goods necessary to survive. More importantly, on a theoretical level, the pleasure that is at the heart of the human experience, and that ultimately leads to concern for others, begins as a legitimate concern for the self and its own satisfaction.

The central Jewish story about the miracle of human consciousness is that of the Garden of Eden. In this story, "proto-humans" become real human beings when they exercise their power of moral decision-making. Adam and Eve were permitted to eat from every tree in the Garden except the Tree of the Knowledge of Good and Evil and the Tree of Life. If they had eaten from the latter, they would have achieved immortality. When they did, in fact, violate God's command and eat from the former, they achieved the power of moral choice. It is no accident that this story immediately follows the story of creation. Creation is not complete until people have acquired the knowledge of right and wrong and the ability to choose between them; moral conscience is an integral part of what it means to have been created as human beings. Moreover, since moral decision-making was a power originally reserved only for God, we in fact draw a little bit closer to the Divine by virtue of our ability to choose. Now, only immortality separates us from God. The constitution of human moral consciousness is thus seen as basic to our tradition. Mussar theory will build on this biblical and rabbinic foundation and make this issue of moral choice important in an even more fundamental way.

In Mussar theory, human consciousness is defined as the tension between the *yetzer ha-tov* and the *yetzer ha-ra*. In other words, we are conscious of our own being because of the ever-present choice we have between what is right and what is wrong. Rabbi Moshe Ḥayyim Luzzatto writes in the introduction to *Mesillat Yesharim:*

> I have written this work not to teach people what they do not know, but to remind them of what they already know and is very evident to them. You will find in most of my words only things that most people know and about which they have no doubts. But just as these things are well known and their truths are revealed to all, so too is forgetfulness in relation to them extremely prevalent. It follows, then, that the benefit to be obtained from this work will not be derived from a single reading; for it is possible that readers will find that they have learned little after having read it that they did not know before. Its benefit will be derived, rather, through review and persistent study. In this way, one will be reminded of those things that one is prone to forget by nature, and through which one is caused to take to heart the duty that we tend to overlook.

This paragraph makes three points: (1) there is nothing new to be learned from this book; (2) the problem that the book addresses is forgetfulness; and (3) therefore, the book cannot be read but must be studied. Ramḥal returns to these themes, explicitly and implicitly, over and over again throughout *Mesillat Yesharim*.

The first issue—that one will not learn anything new from the book—can be called "pre-existing ethics." Readers or students of Ramḥal's work must recognize that the general outline of Jewish ethics (understood as obligations) is already contained within the structure of their own consciousness. Where does this pre-existent ethic come from? Ramḥal believes that it derives from two sources: it originates constitutionally in the formation of human consciousness, and it is further developed through the process of communal socialization. All human beings are formed with both a *yetzer ha-tov* and a *yetzer ha-ra,* an inclination for good and an inclination for evil. These abide in and as the structure of human consciousness, substantially defining the meaning of creation in the image and likeness of God. Thus, the human condition necessarily exists in the tension between good and evil. This condition, from which all of our behavior derives, is the meaning not only of our existence but also of existence itself, insofar as our existence is an "image" of existence itself (i.e., of God). The obligation to choose the good, and thereby to assume responsibility for the other in service to God, precedes our consciousness of ourselves.

Ramḥal uses the Hebrew term *meforsam,* "evident," which refers to those ideas that are known to us by virtue of what we can call "natural wisdom." These are truths that we recognize on the basis of our innate ethical sensibility and for which we depend neither on extensive logical argumentation nor on revelation. We refer to this type of "truth" as the constitution of consciousness, as opposed to the content of consciousness. On the other hand, Ramḥal elsewhere asserts that wisdom—that is, the act of choosing the *yetzer ha-tov*—is already implanted in the human soul in the form of the light of the Shekhinah, the immanent presence of God in the world, and all of our intellectual faculties (including imagination and emotional responses) derive from the *yetzer ha-tov.* In addition, says Ramḥal, persistent study and repetitive learning help to correlate the mouth of the human being with the mouth of God, thus actualizing the innate or pre-existent wisdom. The implied purpose of *Mesillat Yesharim* is to provide a method of uniting the various "flames" of the Shekhinah's fire that normally emerge in our various intellectual acts but that remain separate. The literary structure of *Mesillat Yesharim* is intended to facilitate the unification of the Shekhinah's flames within our soul. This can be achieved when persistent, repetitive study helps us to internalize the orderly application of *middot,* character traits.

We "know" about this gift of our consciousness primarily through the processes of socialization. This occurs both through our interactions with other people, who expose us to ourselves through their care for us, and through our formal exposure to the accumulated traditions of wisdom (specifically the Torah), which explicitly acknowledge this gift. At this point we should note that Torah represents not only the inscription of our awareness of our own consciousness as the accumulation of a historical record, but also the inscription of the radical claim of creation itself. Moreover, Torah also describes our response to the call from our consciousness, a call that originates both within it and outside of it. That is to say, Torah is the unfolding of our consciousness of ourselves and, simultaneously, the unfolding of our consciousness and the debt it owes to another, outside of itself.

The second problem that Ramḥal must address is a consequence of our intrinsic and socialized knowledge: what he calls our forgetfulness of this knowledge. In this opening paragraph he does not explain the source of this forgetfulness, which we have been calling "falling asleep" as opposed to "wakefulness." However, as he segues to the third and final problem in this paragraph, he begins to hint at it. Ramḥal suggests that students view this as a book to *study* (rather than as a book simply to read). By reading the book and finding the content familiar, students might feel that they have not learned anything new. We must then conclude that forgetfulness is not remedied by recalling facts to mind, but rather has something to do with what we might call a particular stance in the world and the avoidance of that stance. If knowledge is understood as simply collecting information, then acquiring knowledge will not help us in our struggle against forgetfulness. "Remembering" in Ramḥal's sense has to do more with breaking through the very structures of intellect. The *yetzer ha-ra* uses intellectual rationalizations to deflect the true obligations of consciousness. This cannot be combated by the passivity of reading, but must be combated through an active process that Ramḥal will call study. Much of his book and much Mussar theory is concerned with describing and implementing this process.

The twin concepts of *yetzer ha-tov* and *yetzer ha-ra* are, we must reiterate, absolutely essential to understanding of Mussar theory. These ideas help to define what we mean by human consciousness. We are conscious human beings insofar as we have before us, at every single moment, a choice between good and evil. Our humanity is defined by our awareness of this choice and by how we choose to act when faced with this choice. Obviously, this level of consciousness is not to be confused with the physical acts that sustain our animate nature. It is not the fact that we breathe, eat, drink, or sleep that makes us human. Rather, we grow into our humanity. In this sense, children are not expected to already be fully human, but only potentially human. This theoretical distinction between biological humanity and ethical morality is necessary for understanding moral life. The physical life of all living creatures is sacred. But full consciousness—what we can call "Mussar consciousness"—implies a level of life and maturity beyond the physical. This level of life is defined by our accepting the responsibility of the choice between good and evil that faces us at every moment.

Our parents, teachers, and social institutions bring us to a certain level of human consciousness. Yet Mussar suggests that full consciousness is difficult to attain and even more difficult to sustain. The responsibility for the other person that we described earlier, which constitutes the fullness of Mussar consciousness, causes most of us to block out its full weight. Luzzatto calls this "forgetfulness" and we have called it "sleep." Learning to stay more awake is central to Mussar practice. Learning to stay awake is an issue of character development. Therefore, our tendency to sleep will be addressed primarily through attention to our character traits. But what are those traits, and where and how are they formed in the human soul? In the next chapter, we will turn our attention to two more important terms of Mussar theory, which require definition before we can answer those questions.

CHAPTER FIVE

Yirat Hashem and Ahavat Hashem

The two primary tools that people use to orient themselves toward the *yetzer ha-tov* and away from the *yetzer ha-ra,* according to Mussar theory, are *yirat hashem,* usually translated as "fear of God," and *ahavat hashem,* or "love of God." Once again we will turn to Rabbi Moshe Ḥayyim Luzzatto to begin our consideration of these terms. He writes in the introduction to *Mesillat Yesharim:*

If we do not look into and analyze the question of what constitutes true fear of God and what its ramifications are, how will we acquire it and how will we escape worldly vanity, which renders our hearts forgetful of it? Will it not be forgotten and get lost even though we recognize its necessity? Love of God, too—if we do not make an effort to implant it in our hearts, utilizing all of the means that direct us toward it, how will it exist within us? Whence will enter our soul passionate intimacy toward the Blessed One and toward Torah if we do not give heart to God's greatness and majesty, which engender this intimacy in our hearts? How will our thoughts be purified if we do not strive to rescue them from imperfections infused in them by physical nature? And all of the character traits, which are in such great need of correction and cultivation—who will cultivate and correct them if we do not give heart to them and subject them to exacting scrutiny? If we analyzed the matter honestly, would we not extract the truth and thereby benefit ourselves, and also be of benefit to others by instructing them in it? As stated by Solomon: "If you seek it as silver and search for it as treasure, then you will understand the fear of God (Proverbs 2:4)." He does not say, "Then you shall understand philosophy; then you will understand medicine; then you will understand legal judgments and decisions." We see, then, that for fear of God to be understood, it must be sought as silver and searched for as treasure. All this is part of our heritage and accepted in substance by every devout individual.

Acquiring *yirat hashem* and *ahavat hashem* is, for Luzzatto, absolutely crucial; the perfection of our character traits depends on having these tools, as does any hope we have for attaining an intimate relationship with God. It is not easy to inculcate these values within ourselves, and we must expend significant effort to seek out these precious attributes.

As explained in the previous chapter, consciousness is constituted on the tension between *yetzer ha-tov* and *yetzer ha-ra*. To help us negotiate this tension and resolve it, we must examine the concepts of *yirat hashem* and *ahavat hashem* more closely. Both *yirat hashem* and *ahavat hashem* come to us from outside ourselves. They are quintessentially intersubjective: they involve us with another. Also, they must be actively sought. Effort must be expended if we are to attain these qualities.

There is an unmistakable connection between our work on attaining the states of *yirat hashem* and *ahavat hashem,* on the one hand, and our work in developing our character traits, or *middot,* on the other hand. Working on the *middot* develops both *yirat hashem* and *ahavat hashem*. The development of *yirat hashem* and *ahavat hashem,* in turn, orients us toward the *yetzer ha-tov* along the line of tension between *yetzer ha-ra* and *yetzer ha-tov.* It is this relation that justifies and motivates our concern with character: it leads us to a more accurate experience of ourselves. Ramḥal continues:

Again, is it conceivable that we should find time for all other branches of study and none for this study? Why should people not at least set aside certain times for this speculation if they are obliged in the remainder of their time to turn to other studies or undertakings? Scripture states, "*Hen* fear of God—this is wisdom" (Job 28:28). Our Sages of blessed memory comment, "*Hen* means 'one,' for in Greek 'one' is designated as *hen*" (Sanhedrin 31b). We see, then, that fear, and only fear, is considered to be wisdom. And there is no doubt that what entails no analysis is not considered wisdom. The truth of the matter is that all of these things require great analysis if they are to be known in truth and not merely through imagination and deceitful supposition. How much the more so if they are to be acquired and attained! One who inquires into these matters will see that saintliness does not hinge upon those things that are put at a premium by the foolishly "saintly," but rather upon true perfection and great wisdom. This is what Moses our teacher, may peace be upon him, teaches us in saying, "And now, Israel, what does Adonai your God ask of you, but that you fear Adonai your God to walk in all God's ways, to love God and serve Adonai your God with all your heart and all your soul, to observe the *mitzvot* of Adonai and God's statutes . . ." (Deuteronomy 10:12). In this verse have been included all of the features of perfection of divine service that are appropriate in relation to the Holy Blessed One. They are: fear of God, walking in God's ways, love, wholeheartedness, and observance of all of the *mitzvot*.

Yirat hashem is understood by Ramḥal as synonymous with wisdom. We have already seen that the tension between the *yetzer ha-tov* and the *yetzer ha-ra* are the essential constitution of human consciousness, and it is our consciousness of our consciousness—our consciousness of our relation to the *yetzer ha-ra* and the *yetzer ha-tov*—that *yirat hashem* and *ahavat hashem* can come to facilitate. These terms describe something that is called into existence in our consciousness from outside, giving us the gift of our own consciousness. This is the function of wisdom in the classical sense: Wisdom is that which exists outside of ourselves, yet enables us to heighten our own awareness of ourselves.

For Luzzatto, however, wisdom means something slightly different. It is understood as the faculty we possess as a gift of God through which we implement the choices we make every day, of whether to follow our *yetzer ha-ra* or our *yetzer ha-tov.* The ethical choice between good and evil describes the very constitution of our consciousness. The seriousness of this choice and its ubiquity fill us with a feeling of trepidation. We tremble with the knowledge that at every moment we are in a position to choose between good and evil. We are sometimes terrified by this choice, to the extent that we refuse to recognize it and take action. However, not to recognize the choice is, of course, also to make a choice— namely, to feign sleep in the face of the ethical dilemmas that define every moment of human time. The term *yirat hashem* describes this trembling before our responsibilities. We are indeed afraid: not afraid of some image of a punishing parent (despite the fact that the tradition often uses such imagery), but rather we are terrified of our responsibilities that are always with us and of the consequences of not meeting those responsibilities.

Yirat hashem also has another meaning. The fear that we have just described of the terrifying choice that confronts us as human beings is traditionally called *yirat ha-onesh,* or "fear of punishment,"

though we've interpreted it more accurately as the fear of the ramifications of our failure to meet our responsibilities. But another
meaning of *yirah* is expressed by the concept *yirat ha-romemut,*
probably best expressed as "fear (or awe) in the presence of the
majesty of God." Luzzatto describes this second aspect of fear in
these words:

> "Fear of God" denotes fear of the majesty of the Blessed One, fearing
> God as one would fear a great and mighty king, and being ashamed at
> one's every movement in consequence of God's greatness, especially
> while speaking before God in prayer or engaging in the study of Torah.

These two types of fear are related but are not the same. Fear of
God is a fear engendered not by God's power but by God's
"majesty," which means God's infinity or what we might call God's
transcendence. Relative to God, we are powerfully aware of our
own mortality and the necessity of satisfying our needs. *Yirat ha-
romemut* is a reminder that when compared to God's unlimited
nature, our own needs are actually quite limited in scope. God's
call upon us is unlimited. Our desire to do good for our unlimited
or Infinite Beloved causes us to feel ashamed in God's presence,
when we consider our obsessions with our own needs.

The second focus of our ethical consciousness is *ahavat hashem,*
the love of God. Both *yirah* and *ahavah* describe the fact that our
consciousness is fundamentally predicated on relationships. The
quality of these relationships is described as the necessary interdependence of our consciousnesses. Love is, initially, the experience
of something outside of ourselves. The love that we receive from
those who care for and nurture us imbues us, in turn, with the
desire to reciprocate this love. We are first the objects of love and
then we become the subjects of love, the lovers. As lovers, our love
first focuses on those closest to us, our parents. However, it eventu-

ally extends to others, our lovers, and it is still not exhausted. In fact, we discover that our desire to love is an infinite desire and can only be fully satisfied when be directed toward an Infinite Beloved, namely God. The infinite love for the Infinite Beloved commands us to do that which is pleasing to our beloved. In the case of God, that which is pleasing is choosing to follow the *yetzer ha-tov*. Love is the source of commandment. Ramḥal explains this concept as follows:

> "Love"—that there be implanted in a person's heart a love for the Blessed One, which will arouse one's soul to do what is pleasing before God, just as one's heart is aroused to give pleasure to one's father and mother. One will be grieved at the lack of this in oneself or in others; they will be jealous for it and rejoice greatly in fulfilling it in any way.

Yirat hashem and *ahavat hashem* are the primary means for the expression of human choice between the *yetzer ha-ra* and the *yetzer ha-tov.* But both *yirah* and *ahavah* are determined, on a practical level, by paying attention to the *middot,* the character traits that express either of these two primary tools in our day-to-day lives. We will deal extensively with the *middot* in the third section of this book.

CHAPTER SIX

Kibbush Ha-Yetzer
and Tikkun Ha-Yetzer

If we are able to achieve an appropriate attitude of *yirah*, we should then be able to overcome the challenges presented to us by our *yetzer ha-ra*. If we are successful in this endeavor, what then happens to the *yetzer ha-ra* in our consciousness? If human consciousness is, indeed, constructed along the tension between the *yetzer ha-ra* and the *yetzer ha-tov*, does our ability to overcome the *yetzer ha-ra* then entail the disappearance of this tension? The simple answer to this question is: No. The *yetzer ha-ra* is an integral part of our nature and can never disappear completely. To understand what ideally happens to the *yetzer ha-ra*, given that it cannot disappear, we turn our attention to two concepts articulated by Rav Yisrael Salanter. These are *kibbush ha-yetzer*, the first step of suppressing the *yetzer*, and *tikkun ha-yetzer*, the second step of transforming the *yetzer*.

In Mussar practice, one must choose a particular *middah*, or character trait, to strengthen in one's personality. In order to integrate this trait into one's actions, Mussar practice would have one use a verse or saying that reminds one of the *middah* and of the desired behavior. Focusing on this verse can heighten awareness of the *middah* and the behavior, and hopefully serve to change one's actions in the desired direction, in contradistinction to one's unmediated impulse. With the application of this remedy, over time, one's actions can and do change. However, the impulse toward less desirable behavior remains, and this process of controlling or suppressing the action continues to be necessary.

Kibbush ha-yetzer can enable a person to reach an even higher level of ethical-spiritual accomplishment than what we have described in the previous paragraph. Suppressing unwanted actions can, over time, become habitual; this can, in fact, result in the suppression of the impulse itself. One can become so accustomed to suppressing unwanted behavior that the habit of doing so gradually reduces even the impulse itself. However, it is always possible for the impulse to reassert itself and, under conditions of particular stress or temptation, even the unwanted behavior may reappear. Thus the ability to achieve *kibbush ha-yetzer* requires vigilance and ongoing practice in order to forestall a return of the behavior. To this end, Rav Salanter suggests that a person should continue using the strategies of *kibbush* even after the behavior seems to have disappeared. If one has found a verse that successfully addresses a particular behavior, one should continue to include it in an ongoing review of such strategies. For example, one might be actively working on controlling impulse buying, which is a violation of the *middah* of frugality. Such a person may already have engaged in strenuous spiritual exercise in order to control a different *middah,* such as orderliness. If, for example, they have passionately studied verses in Genesis about the order of creation and memorized some of those texts, then calling the verses to mind when confronted with the impulse to disorderliness may, in fact, remind them of the *middah* of orderliness, helping them to be more successful in keeping personal items well ordered, keeping appointments, etc. This person should continue to review these lessons and verses about orderliness briefly, after working more strenuously on the *middah* of frugality, even imagining scenarios to which they might be exposed that might cause the *yetzer* to reassert the impulse to disorder.

However, an even higher order of spiritual accomplishment requires *tikkun ha-yetzer,* the transformation of the impulse from negative to positive. This is the highest level of behavioral transformation that Mussar practice can achieve. It is accomplished by an intense contemplation of one's *middot,* until the very impulse to do evil is transformed into energy for doing good. Rav Salanter writes in *Ohr Yisrael,* his collected writings:

> . . . One should transform one's emotional forces and character traits for the good, until the power of evil is entirely uprooted from within oneself. In this area, it does not suffice to correct one's will in a general manner, to make oneself desire good and hate evil. Rather, a person must seek out the way to correct each individual character trait and emotional force. This aspect of rectification refers to the rational *mitzvot* that are between a person and their fellow. (Letter 30)

This level of character transformation requires a simultaneous transformation of all of one's *middot.* In his early writings, Rav Salanter suggested that such a transformation was more likely in a young person than in an older person, and should therefore ideally precede *kibbush* programmatically. Training a young person in *tikkun* could thus obviate the need for *kibbush.* Conversely, one untrained in *tikkun* as a youth could accrue sufficient life experience to do a better job of *kibbush* as an older person. Later Salanter reversed his position, seeming to recognize that *kibbush* had to precede *tikkun* regardless of age. I believe that this latter understanding of the relationship between the two concepts is correct.

We have here discussed the concepts of *kibbush ha-yetzer* and *tikkun ha-yetzer,* and we will deal more extensively with the possibility of both *kibbush* and *tikkun ha-middot* when we deal with the practice of *middah* improvement in the next section. Our purpose here has been to introduce the terms and, by doing so, to consider the options that Mussar makes available to us in choosing between the *yetzer ha-ra* and the *yetzer ha-tov.* Clearly, Rav Salanter was very much aware of the depth of the problem, and the depths of the human soul that are engaged in this choice. He was also aware of a web of solutions, enabling one to set realistic goals over a period of time for addressing these challenges.

CHAPTER SEVEN

Olam Ha-Zeh, Olam Ha-Ba, and Reward and Punishment

I

The terms *olam ha-zeh,* this world, and *olam ha-ba,* the world to come, are twin terms forming an essential part of traditional Jewish theology as well as Mussar theology and theory. Strictly speaking, these terms refer to two "places" in which the human experience unfolds. These two places may indeed be co-existent; however, our personal experience of them is chronologically determined. That is, the world to come and this world both already exist. But for now, only someone no longer in this world, someone who is dead, can experience the world to come. Conversely, one will only experience the world to come when they exit this world, when they die. Although this world and the world to come exist simultaneously, our experience of the world to come always lies in our future.

Moreover, the traditional concept of *olam ha-zeh* sees it as a material world. Generally speaking this is contrasted with *olam ha-ba,* which is conceived as a spiritual world. While there is and can be no dispute regarding the material nature of *olam ha-zeh,* the picture is more complex than it first appears, as the spiritual nature of *olam ha-ba* is not entirely clear.

Regarding *olam ha-ba,* two other concepts must be introduced: *yemot ha-mashiah,* messianic days, and, *tehiyat ha-metim,* resurrection of the dead. What is the relationship between these eschatological events and *olam ha-ba?* Do they occur within the realm of *olam ha-zeh,* or do they mark the boundary between *olam ha-zeh* and *olam ha-ba?* Or do they take place entirely within *olam ha-ba?* Furthermore, is the resurrection of the dead a physical event or a spiritual event? Does it involve bodies as we know them from our world, or are we dealing with a new, perhaps refined, idea of the body—a spiritual body of sorts? Matters are further complicated by the fact that the bodies we do know, our bodies in *olam ha-zeh,* are themselves not entirely material in nature. Our this–worldly embodiedness includes a part of us that is not usually thought of as being material: our consciousness or soul. Are the dead to be revived as bodies and souls both, or only as souls? The answers to these questions directly impact our ability to create a topological map of the scope of human life, spanning both *olam ha-zeh* and *olam ha-ba.*

We can best address these eschatological concerns if we frame them as answers to questions, which belong in the realm of sophisticated religious insight. While the answers to the questions attempt to describe *olam ha-ba,* we take for granted that we cannot know anything definitive about *olam ha-ba,* empirically. No one gets to go there and return to describe the experience. Therefore, the answers to the following list of philosophical questions should not be seen as definitive, but instead they are intended to carve out a space for meaning.

1. How is the idea of the future derived?
2. In light of futurity, how is time measured?
3. What is the meaning of materiality?

4. What is the meaning of spirituality?
5. How is the past derived and is it a material or spiritual dimension?

The most logical place to begin our investigation of these questions is in the present. Even though the question seems obvious, we must ask it: What is the present? It is not uncommon for people to suggest that the present is nothing more than an intellectual construct, that no actual present exists. Since every moment passes into the past before it can be reflected upon and life pushes forward unrelentingly, perhaps only the past and future exist in any truly meaningful way. The present, some would argue, is only either a memory or an expectation. However, this conventional wisdom is inaccurate.

On the contrary, we always experience time in the present. We carry ourselves from moment to moment, and as we do we fill the space that might otherwise belong to the past or to the future. In fact, the present is entirely about us, about me. Being in the present is about experiencing my feelings, my needs and my wants, my meeting those needs, and the satisfaction that brings me. In the present there can be no room for anyone else, because in order to make room for someone else I would have to postpone my own satisfaction. In this postponement another person's needs would take priority over my own. I would then have to wait for some time in the future—perhaps only an hour, or perhaps for tomorrow, or perhaps indefinitely. It doesn't matter how long I have to wait; waiting for another creates the future for me.

Thus our initial experience of the present is actually as lack of time or timelessness, the very opposite of eternity. Eternity is the endless future time, but the present is bereft of time. Bearing our weight—focusing exclusively on ourselves—precludes time, which can only begin when I have to wait for another. Time is a function of my relationship with another, as Levinas first worked out in *Time and the Other*. Similarly, the biblical story of creation intimates that time commences only with the establishment of a relationship between the One and another, between God and something outside of God ("*When* God began to create the heavens and the earth . . ." [Genesis 1:1]).

Is the future a material or a spiritual dimension? In other words, if the future is created by displacing myself with another, is this a physical or a spiritual displacement? To respond to this question, however, we must break down the overly-simplistic duality between the "I" and the "other." The "I" who is displaced while waiting for another is a spiritual entity. It is a spiritual consciousness that processes the time of waiting, thus creating the future. Nevertheless, the displacement itself is of one body by another body. It is the physical presence of another—their persistence, their filling the space of themselves—that displaces our own presence, making it our future. This displacement, this ceding of space, is indeed a physical act, even if we call it psychological. What displaces us, what forces us to wait for them, is their materiality. The future is my waiting for—and on—my neighbor's materiality. In waiting for them we are also waiting *on* them, serving them. We are feeding them.

There is, then, a relationship that refuses to sever the spiritual and the material aspects of being. It is a relationship so complex that a single image or idiom will not do it justice. The relationship between the body and the spirit cannot be rendered simply in Jewish thought. It requires a complex combination of ideas, which may themselves be neither necessarily logically consistent nor mutually exclusive.

In considering the present, we have come to understand more about the nature of time, particularly as it relates to the future. Indeed, time does not exist in the present; each moment of the present is experienced as being the same, weighted down by the all-encompassing ego. However, when the "I" moves aside to make room for another, we then experience time, as the future comes into existence for us. When our relationship with another frees us of our own overwhelming weight, time can even fly by. The nature of our service to another will determine the experience we have of time. But time will always be a paradoxical experience: no matter how quickly time passes, we are, by definition, always waiting. Time is always the time of the other person. The desire we have to serve that other person evolves toward the infinite and requires an Infinite Beloved. Thus our waiting is equally infinite.

We have made progress in answering the questions posed above. We now understand the idea of the future and we also understand time in the light of futurity. Moreover, we recognize that the present and the future require a mixture of materiality and spirituality. What remains to be investigated are the final two questions, regarding the possibility of a pure spirituality and the relationship of such a spirituality to the past. The possibility of a pure spirituality depends on our understanding of the past, which will in turn be derived from our understanding of the present and the future. If there exists a domain of pure spirit, that would represent a dimension with a claim on the present for which the weight of the present must make room, but for which it does not have to wait. Neither the present nor the future can be purely spiritual until they have a past to anchor them. The ultimate destination of both the present and the future is the past, as inconceivable as that may sound. In fact, the immateriality of the past is experienced only as memory, even as memories that we could not have experienced ourselves, personally. Such memories are conveyed to us via language that we can grasp only as revelation. As Jews we call that revelation and its sustaining literature Torah.

We have considered the philosophical questions that elicit traditional theological answers regarding eschatology. This process directed our attention to the immaterial past toward which both the present and the future are infinitely tending: toward the revelation of Torah. That past compels the ego to make room for it, and thus prepares the way to make room for the future. We now return to the terminology with which we began our inquiry, in order to re-appropriate that vocabulary as our own.

It should now be clear that *olam ha-zeh* and *olam ha-ba* must exist simultaneously, since the present and the future are in fact the same place. What differentiates them is the displacement of the ego that turns the former into the latter. However, the self can only be displaced permanently by death. Thus, the fullest attainment of *olam ha-ba* can be achieved only through death. However, in a less extreme understanding, *olam ha-zeh* and *olam ha-ba* otherwise describe the relationship between the self and another. No person can be expected to displace their needs permanently. But to the extent that one can displace those needs in order to serve another, one can then move back and forth between *olam ha-zeh* and *olam ha-ba*. This possibility of traveling between *olam ha-zeh* and *olam ha-ba* is crucial. Levinas attributes this understanding to the teaching of Rabbi Ḥayyim of Volozhin, and it is found also in the writings of Rav Simḥa Zissel and Rav Moshe Ḥayyim Luzzatto (as discussed in this book). Whether one is in one world or the other is a direct function of the level of responsibility for another that one is willing and able to bear.

The nature of *olam ha-ba*, whether it is a world of spirit or of matter is, as we've seen, enormously complex. This world and the world to come permeate one another; the spiritual nature of my own future depends on my assuming responsibility for the material nature of my neighbor. Therefore, the world to come unfolds in both a physical dimension and a spiritual dimension. The physical dimension of the world to come is expressed by the idea of *teḥiyat ha-metim,* the bodily resurrection of the dead. For Jews, belief in *teḥiyat ha-metim* allows us to keep in mind the materiality of our neighbor's needs, and to hold the unrelenting demands of those material needs close to our hearts. *Teḥiyat ha-metim* is thus the necessary material component of the world of the future.

The world to come is not only my future, as we've seen; it is my future ever cognizant of an impossible-to-experience past that is, nevertheless, my past. We have characterized this impossible past as a revelation, as Torah. Revelation in its role as the future's past, however, is a past that has not yet occurred—an impossibly future past even more impossible than the impossible past of the past. *Yemot ha-mashiaḥ,* messianic time, lies beyond and impossibly "after" *olam ha-ba*—although on this construction, chronology becomes almost meaningless. This is, to use language we introduced above, the impossible time of wakefulness. The possibility of wakefulness in the future redirects the very notion of time around to meet its beginning in the past. It is the moment of beginning, experienced as the moment of endless beginning. It is Moses and Israel at Sinai, accepting responsibility for every creature and, at the same moment, meeting that responsibility. It is the future of the other, and the present of the self, and the past of both—all experienced simultaneously, and thus transforming the very nature of time beyond our ability to express it. This is *yemot ha-mashiaḥ,* messianic time.

II

In the Jewish imagination, the subject of reward and punishment is closely related to the subject of eschatology. The world to come is commonly conceived of as the reward, or perhaps as the place for meting out either reward or punishment. The concepts of reward and punishment play a major role in traditional Mussar theory and they need to be addressed in the context of a contemporary Mussar theory.

These concepts will be easier to consider after having already investigated the concepts of *olam ha-zeh* and *olam ha-ba*. We have already shown that this world and the world to come are co-existent. We have also shown that the world to come is precisely the future that awaits all those who are able to make room in their lives for the material needs of another person. In this sense, then, *olam ha-ba* is precisely the reward for acts that reflect accepting responsibility for another. Conversely, those who refuse to accept this responsibility forfeit the world to come.

This understanding is not simply substituting an intellectual concept of punishment for a physical one. Although physical punishment may seem more menacing, the pain of being trapped in the present is nonetheless very real. To use Levinas's term, the "enchainment" to one's ego does have material consequences. To the extent that one would have absolutely no responsibility to another human being, one is deprived of more than merely a future. One is deprived of time, joy, love, learning, care, nurture, and sustenance—because all of these human benefits require some level of inter-subjectivity. To be absolutely without these things certainly is to be in hell, deprived of both a future and a past. If this world and the world to come exist simultaneously, then this world and the possibility of losing the world to come also exist simultaneously.

Mercifully, the absolute loss of the world to come is another near impossibility, which we can only begin to imagine in the most extreme of cases. God's mercy is such that almost all human beings must assume some responsibility for themselves and also accept at least some responsibility for another. The merciful balm of accepting a little responsibility for another has a powerfully healing effect on us. Thus, one does not have to accept very much responsibility in order to already feel some degree of good, which is the reward of the world to come. This feeling of good, however, is at once both a reward and a challenge. The fact that doing so little can make us feel good may remove the incentive for us to do even more, in order to feel even more good. It could mislead us into thinking that we have achieved our goals long before we have actually achieved them. This is precisely the problem with which this book began, and with which many of the classics of Mussar literature are concerned: What prevents me from doing what is good? Often, what prevents us from doing *more* good is the merciful reward we receive for doing just a *little* good. Mussar awakens us to how much others are still in pain, and how much responsibility remains for us to take up. It promises a much greater reward in the true world to come than we have already tasted in this world.

PART THREE

Contemporary
Mussar Practice

CHAPTER EIGHT

Shiur—Learning

Mussar practice can be divided into six major areas of action: the *shiur*, or learning session; *ḥeshbon ha-nefesh*, or accounting of the soul; the *va'ad*, or group processing; *hitpa'alut*, or intense verbal intervention; *hashgaḥah*, or private counseling; *derekh eretz*, or wordly wisdom, and *mazkeh ha-rabbim*, teaching Mussar to others. In this chapter we will deal with the *shiur* and other aspects of Mussar practice will be addressed in subsequent chapters.

There is a well-known story in Mussar circles of the moment of spiritual awakening that occurred in the life of the founder of the movement, Rav Yisrael of Salant. According to the story, Rav Yisrael was attracted in his youth to a pious and reclusive figure in the town of Salant, Rav Yosef Zundal—so much so that young Yisrael would follow Rav Yosef around as the latter wandered through the forests near the town immersed in contemplation. Yisrael would overhear Rav Yosef reflecting with particular fervor, raising his voice and shaking his body as he repeated various statements from his study with the intent to memorize and to rouse himself to more demanding ethical action. It is unknown how long Rav Yosef was aware of the young student shadowing him, but on one particular day Rav Zundal turned to Yisrael and said to him: "Yisrael, learn Mussar and you will become a *yerei shamayim* (one imbued with fear of heaven)." An accomplished *yeshiva* student, Yisrael would have known that Rav Yosef was directing him to delve into the traditional texts of Mussar, which were well known but generally neglected in favor of talmudic studies. At the same time Rav Yosef's behavior provided Salanter with a model for Mussar learning. He studied with Rav Yosef for a short time before the latter relocated to Israel, by which time Salanter had begun to develop the principles that he would eventually develop into the Mussar movement. Foremost among those principles was what we might call rescuing, or at least restoring spiritual importance to, Mussar literature. While he valued traditional study of Torah and Talmud, Salanter believed that such study alone was ultimately futile. Thus he championed the legitimacy of Mussar as a complementary study of the literature that nurtured souls concerned with *yirat hashem* and concerned with the weighty responsibility of choosing the *yetzer ha-tov* over the *yetzer ha-ra*. To borrow from what we learned from Levinas, one's search for knowledge had to begin with ethics, or else law or philosophy would not matter at all.

When we talk about the *shiur* in contemporary Mussar practice we are basing ourselves on the same literature that Rav Salanter promoted. This study need not necessarily take place in a group. Although the study of Mussar literature in private is certainly salutary, we prefer the idea of the study group, led by an experienced teacher, for three important reasons. First, Rav Salanter insisted that Mussar learning was most efficacious when conducted at a fixed time: the *shiur* asks people to make a commitment to others when scheduling their Mussar study. Busy people are more likely to uphold a regular commitment to study when they have made a commitment to other people, and not only to themselves.

Second, the *shiur* facilitates *hitpa'alut* (see chapter 10). Developing the intensity in our study conducive to the process of changing our behavior is more easily accomplished in a group setting. Third, the *shiur* provides for a relationship between students and teacher, which can serve as a model for developing Mussar consciousness.

The content of the *shiur* is always a text from the treasury of Mussar literature. There are a number of such texts that recommend themselves, such as *Mesillat Yesharim* by Rabbi Moshe Hayyim Luzzatto, *Hokhmah U-Mussar* by Rabbi Simha Zissel Braude of Kelm, and the collected writings of Rav Yisrael Salanter, *Ohr Yisrael*. These are all available in English translation[1] except for *Hokhmah U-Mussar,* a partial translation of which is included in the appendix to this book.

Whatever material is chosen for study, and whether it is studied in a group or individually, Rav Salanter insisted that Mussar texts be studied with "lips aflame"—that is, aloud. The text should be read aloud and with sufficient passion to make the reader or listener feel as though their intellectual defenses were being assaulted. Only when these defenses are softened by the regular study of Mussar texts is it possible to achieve the spiritual motivation necessary to engage in the real work of Mussar yet to come—namely, effecting change in one's actions and behavior. Rav Salanter established in his day an institution called *Bet Ha-mussar,* the Mussar study house, which was open twenty-four hours a day, and which students could frequent to study Mussar texts aloud, individually or in groups, at any time of the day or night. While such a model is not available to the contemporary Mussar student, it is still possible to engage in regular Mussar study, even for a few minutes a day. This textual under-

---

[1] *The Path of the Just,* Torah Classics Library, Feldheim Publishers, Yosef Liebling, trans. 2004. *Ohr Yisrael: The Writings of Rav Yisrael Salanter,* Targum/Feldheim Publishers, 2004.

pinning of the Mussar discipline is so essential that Rav Salanter insisted on establishing a regular, fixed time for the study of Mussar every day. Obviously, establishing a fixed time for Mussar study accomplishes a number of desirable goals. First, in addition to the exhortation one receives from the text itself, one begins to learn how to establish order—which, as we will see shortly, is a critical *middah*. Second, by establishing and maintaining a fixed time for Mussar study, one establishes a time during the day when one cannot be involved in choosing to do evil in any way. Thus the regularity of study establishes a small base for the eventual development of a regularity of positive *middah* behavior, since "order" is one of the *middot* to be worked on. Most importantly, regular, fixed Mussar study impels us to be involved not only in study but also in the *middah* work that it introduces by providing a more inviting point of entry to our daily Mussar work than would be provided by proceeding immediately to the more difficult, behavioral component of *middah* work without text-study serving to ease that transition.

CHAPTER NINE

Ḥeshbon Ha-Nefesh—
An Accounting of the Soul

The Va'ad and the Middot

The transformation that Mussar can effect takes place in and through the work of *tikkun* and *kibbush ha-yetzer*. As explained in chapter 6, *tikkun ha-yetzer*, the transformation of the *yetzer ha-ra*, takes many years of dedicated Mussar work. However, in the present context, it is important to recall that a person can reach a very high level of spiritual–ethical consciousness even in the short term, as the process of *kibbush* is refined. Merely suppressing evil impulses can, if ingrained as habitual behavior, completely remove the impulse under normal circumstances. Our Mussar discipline aims to establish this habit of proper behavior in service to others. And it is through the rectification of the character traits that *kibbush* is accomplished.

In order to begin to explore the practical nature of *middah* work we begin with a chart that describes the *middot*. One should note that there is more than one such list of character traits in Mussar literature. The one we have selected, the thirteen *middot* (character traits) as outlined by Rabbi Mendel of Satanov in his book *Ḥeshbon Ha-nefesh,* is recommended by Rav Yisrael Salanter and has been one of the most widely used. There is a good deal of overlap between other lists and this one, and no single list can include all of the nuances of character that may need rectification. As one progresses in *middah* work, one becomes aware of additional areas of character that may require work, even when those areas may be so subtle as to resist naming.

1.	Equanimity	*Menuḥat Ha-nefesh*	Rise above events that are inconsequential—both bad and good—for they are not worth disturbing your equanimity.
2.	Patience	*Savlanut*	When something bad happens to you and you do not have the power to avoid it, do not aggravate the situation even more through wasted grief.
3.	Order	*Seder*	All of your actions and possessions should be orderly—each and every one having a set place and a set time. Let your thoughts always be free to deal with that which lies ahead of you.
4.	Decisiveness	*Ḥaritzut*	All of your acts should be preceded by deliberation; when you have reached a decision, act without hesitating.
5.	Cleanliness	*Nekiyut*	Let no stain or ugliness be found in your possessions or in your home, and surely not on your body or clothes.
6.	Humility	*Anavah*	Always seek to learn wisdom from every person, to recognize your failings and correct them. In doing so you will learn to stop thinking about your virtues and you will take your mind off your fellow's faults.
7.	Righteousness	*Tzedek*	What is hateful to you, do not do to your neighbor.
8.	Frugality	*Kimmutz*	Be careful with your money. Do not spend even a penny needlessly.
9.	Diligence	*Zerizut*	Always find something to do—for yourself or for a friend—and do not allow a moment of your life to be wasted.

10. Silence	*Shetikah*	Before you open your mouth, be silent and reflect: "What benefit will my speech bring to me or to others?"
11. Calmness	*Niḥuta*	The words of the wise are stated gently. In being good, do not be called evil.
12. Truth	*Emet*	Do not allow anything to pass your lips that you are not certain is completely true.
13. Separation	*Perishut*	Strengthen yourself so that you can stop lewd thoughts. Draw close to your [spouse] only when your mind is free, [occupied only] by thoughts of fulfilling your conjugal duties and procreating.

The following is a very brief outline of how the we do the *middah* work individually and as a *va'ad*.

1. Commit yourself to the study of Mussar for at least thirteen weeks. Work on each of the thirteen *middot* above for one week.

2. On awakening, remember the *middah* on which you are currently working. Recite a phrase that you have found, in Scripture or in the *siddur* or even from other literary sources, to help you remember that *middah*.

3. Set a specific time and place for daily Mussar work by yourself. Late at night or early in the morning, when most other people are asleep, may be a time of least distraction. Whatever time you set, keep it consistently. Use the time to review your previous day in terms of your *middah* goal. As part of your reflection the following steps are important:

4. Focus on how your practice of your *middah* affects others in your life.

5. Keep a daily journal in which you record an incident or two from the day that showed when you did (or did not) apply the *middah* of the week.

6. Engage in private study of Torah, Tanakh, Talmud, and the works of Jewish spiritual writers. Examine these texts through the lens of your *middah*.

7. Keep a journal in which you write quotable passages from books

that you are reading, along with your reflections on those passages.
Record phrases that you find in your reading that you can recite to
help you to remember your *middah*.

This outline describes the daily personal work that must be
undertaken in the practice of Mussar, in addition to learning Mussar texts as described in chapter 7. In that chapter we emphasized
the importance of learning in a *shiur,* a group lesson, whenever
possible. When there is a Mussar *shiur,* then the same group can
function as a *va'ad*—that is, a workshop to monitor members'
progress (or lack thereof) in aligning their behavior during the
week with the goals of the particular *middah* or character trait that
the group has chosen to focus on. The group's self-scrutiny is facil-
itated by keeping Mussar/*middot* journals. Each member is required
to choose a Mussar moment, a fixed time each day to do the work
of introspection, and then to share the results of this introspective
work with the *va'ad.*

Mutual support and constructive criticism are offered by the
group members under the supervision of a trained group leader.
Group members are encouraged to find for themselves appropriate
verbal cues, whether quotations from Scripture, traditional texts, or
even secular texts. These are to be memorized and used by group
members to remind themselves of their obligations regarding each
middah throughout the course of the week. In order to deepen the
group's members' connection to Mussar and their Mussar group
during the course of the week, members agree to a weekly study
appointment with a *hevruta* (study partner). This entails a 15- to
30-minute text study session in which the members are expected
to generate questions to be brought back to the *shiur* that precedes
the *va'ad.* The *shiur* and *va'ad* always go together. In the *va'ad* part
of the meeting, members report on whether they have met their
responsiblilities for the week—namely: daily Mussar work, daily

Torah study, and weekly *hevruta*. The *va'ad* becomes, in a sense, the model of the "other" to whom each member is responsible. Once each member has reported, a member of the *va'ad* is asked to share their experience about the particular *middah* during the week. Was it particularly difficult? Did the person experience a sense of success in controlling their behavior in regard to the *middah*? And most importantly, did control of the *middah* result in a measurable impact in service to another? As feelings of trust and safety increase among members of the *va'ad,* the support and criticism of the members can be profoundly helpful to each member in focusing on the work at hand.

CHAPTER TEN

Hitpa'alut and Studying
with Lips Aflame

Rav Yisrael Salanter introduced into the study of Mussar a number of techniques aimed at transforming a primarily intellectual process into an affective one, so that we could break through our intellectual defenses, which protect us from making real changes in our lives, in order to affect behavior. Among these techniques was the use of music, especially *niggunim* or melodies that could accompany the study of Mussar texts. Another technique was *hitpa'alut,* the intense study of particular texts (such as biblical and rabbinic passages) that would address particular moral failings of the student. We have already discussed some of these techniques in earlier sections. But we are returning to these techniques in order to more fully describe the ways in which they can be used in contemporary Mussar practice.

Hitpa'alut begins by selecting a particular text that addresses an identified area of Mussar concern of the student. The student then studies this text aloud, preferably in an emotional mode. For example, a *niggun* might be used to suggest the depth of the student's sorrow at needing to study the text or to reflect the fact that one was still having a problem with a particular *middah.* At its most effective, *hitpa'alut* can lead to an emotional breakthrough, perhaps signified by weeping and trembling, that then begins the process of behavioral change on a profound level.

Achieving this level of emotional connection with the text has always been difficult, but it is even more so today, because we are less familiar with the texts and generally more emotionally reticent with regard to texts. However, we have found that focusing on the text in combination with focusing on our *ḥeshbon ha-nefesh* (accounting of the soul) allows us to become aware of the awesome responsibility that we carry for other people and our inability to carry that responsibility. This often can—and does—precipitate an intense level of emotional response, even to the point of tears, in contemporary Mussar practitioners, especially in the context of the contemporary Mussar *va'ad.*

As described earlier, a Mussar *va'ad* meets weekly following the *shiur* on a Mussar text. Each *va'ad* meeting begins with a "check-in." At this point, each participant reports to the group about whether or not they have kept their Mussar obligations for the week: to set aside fifteen minutes a day for reflection on the *middah* being worked on, to meet weekly with one's *ḥevruta,* and to engage in fifteen minutes of additional Torah study each day. After the participants have checked in it is possible that a discussion will ensue about somebody's failure to meet their responsibilities. The group functions as a model of "the other" to whom each member is responsible.

Following the check-in, the group leader asks the participants if there is anyone who can share their experience with that week's *middah.* This usually precipitates a discussion regarding the nature of the *middah,* its applicability for contemporary life-styles, its difficulties, the impediments individuals experience in implementing it, and, most importantly, the impact on the "others" in one's life depending upon one's character improvement vis-à-vis this *middah*. It is during this discussion that participants may be led by the group to profound insights regarding the material forces *(yetzer ha-ra)* that may be preventing them from living up to their own goals. These realizations can be accompanied by significant emotional responses as well.

The following is a transcript from a *va'ad* session focusing on the *middah* of humility *(anavah)* in which this intensity is apparent. The description of *anavah* taken from Ḥeshbon Ha-nefesh is: "Always seek to learn wisdom from every person, to recognize your failings and correct them. In doing so you will learn to stop thinking about your virtues and you will take your mind off your friend's faults." This is the discussion that ensued in the *va'ad*. (Note: Participants' names are not used; R = Rabbi and C = participant comment.)

C1:   I found this piece of advice to be hardest of all: "Always seek to learn from every person." I really had trouble with this idea. A specific example: there are a couple of people I come into contact with over Shabbat who I find difficult to tolerate, much less learn from—one person, most specifically. I was thinking of the *middah,* and fortunately by thinking of it I didn't have the same strong negative reaction to him that usually overcomes me. I said, "What can I learn from this?" I thought I would walk out of the room when he starts to talk, but then I said, "No, that's not the spirit."

C2:   Can I ask you a question? Maybe this is psychological. This person who pushes your buttons, is it anything in you?

C1:   I don't know, maybe.

C3:   I think there are any number of people who really get on my nerves. . . . When someone gets on my nerves, I say, "Why are they getting on my nerves? What's it about in me?" I've learned that it's probably something in me, something I don't like about myself.

C2:   That is a way to learn from them. I also find that people who get me the most upset are people who are showing some trait of my own—that I don't want to own up to.

C1:   People get on my nerves when I feel like they are too demanding of me. Or maybe it's me, not being able to own up to my obligations to them, as the other.

C2:   Or maybe you want to be more demanding by using a quote to keep centered, so you can learn from a difficult person.

C1:   They may do something that you can't do. For me, it's the person I consider to be my greatest teacher. My ability to be in her presence is always a barometer of where I'm at. She hooks me so totally: what I see in her are ways that I act. She lets parts of herself go that I have but that I don't let go. Then I see her acting that way and I say, "If she can do it, I can do it too"—and then I do that when she's around. I can always tell when I'm around her, if I can see myself acting in a way that I feel good about.

R: What's the mechanism?

C1:   It's the burden of the other. This is a woman I go way back with, through a lot of difficult places in her life. I know enough about her to know her burden, her need. I have to get to the place where I am conscious that she needs something from me and that she will come and get it. I also have to be clear on being positive and giving her attention, but at the same time being strong and centered—because she can knock me off guard easily.

C3:   That was the quote [supplied by a participant], "It takes a lifetime to learn how to be able to hold your own ground, to go out to the others, to be open to them without losing your ground, and to hold your ground without shutting others out."

C2:   That was it!

R: So could you carry that quote around in your heart? Could you use it?

C3:   With lots of practice.

R: So how would you practice?

C3:   I have body poses that I know about, that help me get centered and figure out where I am. I sit in my chair and get conscious of: Are my feet on the ground? Is one foot in front of the other, in an active stance? Am I centered, ready to act, breathing well? I get into position when I'm off, so it helps me remember: Where am I? How am I doing? Am I reacting? What are they doing to me?

R: I remember once having to be with a person who was hysteri-
cal, crying, and he was divesting of a lifetime of pain. I know that
was a difficult place for me, to stay and to be there. How I was
able to accomplish it was with a verse from a psalm: "God heals
the broken-hearted." I wasn't listening to him; I was simply reciting the verse. It felt as though the burden of that emotion was, at
that point, being borne by some other force beside me—so that
I was no longer acting as the recipient. In this situation that
some of you are describing, finding ways to understand that we
are not alone in these encounters might be a helpful tool.

C1:   The person you've been talking about must need to do this in
order to occupy the space, to make himself known.

C2:   That's what I think. I think this person is kind of abusing a position that he has been granted by the *kahal* (community), and he
becomes the actor more concerned with performance than he is
with . . .

R: This raises another issue: How do you avoid being an enabler if
you are taking this role of humility? Do you have no responsibility to confront the other? It's not entirely clear. I would suggest
that sometimes the reason we are so uncomfortable is not that
we are not able to listen, but rather that we are not able to say
what we really think should be said.

C3:   Let's just take the issue of what you brought up, the issue of
kahal, community. It is a system dynamic, with the person acting
in such a way because everyone in the community is colluding
so that he acts that way. That system does not have checks and
balances that keep people functional; that system is distorting this
person's personality. That's the reason that people have in their
mind when they don't say anything to him—at least people who
don't notice him, people who are totally bugged by him, people
who totally love him in the room, I would bet. So in terms of
the system . . .

R: In that case, what you do, perhaps, is to attack the system, and to
suggest there are ways that the system needs to protect itself
from this kind of situation.

C3:   It's not really attacking the system, but rather fixing it.

C2:   It's different from what we learned from the quote that started this conversation.

R: Yes. In a certain sense it's easier than this quote. Despite the system misfires and system remedies, in those situations and situations where there is no system, the ultimate challenge for me is still: How can I look at this person as a teacher? Remember what we just said about teachers. Teachers are pretty important people in this system. We have great deal of obligation to them. If we can transform them into teachers, our relationship with them will change. We will get something which obligates us. Then, if we are obligated, we have a certain love for them. If we can then transform into some kind of love, we will be able to make some progress.

C1:   I have worked with some people who have been jerks, and I have learned from them. I know how to deal with clients, or with people who have technical knowledge. If you don't spend all your time muttering under your breath, you can even learn things from people who are jerks.

R: And being a student of someone, even fleetingly, is an intersubjective experience. It changes them—the teacher—too. There is a sense that every teacher has: If you are teaching and have the sense that your students are hearing you, then there is a shift. It may well be that the key to making this into a relationship and changing it is not only for you, the teacher, to figure out how to learn from the students, but indirectly for them to realize that you are listening.

C3:   There is another level underneath this, I think. People take strong positions because underneath that is fear: fear of not being as powerful as they want to be, fear of not being seen as they want to be seen. Some people who are characterized as jerks and fools have already been made not the other, but they've been made so separate from yourself and humanity. I don't think that's the case. I'm sure there are times when I am a jerk, but I'm struggling not to be that, and in that case it is fear. I saw my lack of humility show up at times when I was most afraid. So, I think there is another way to hold this. Then you can look at how someone reacts to fear, and that is learning because you can say, "Okay, that's not a good way to go."

R: That's what's so profound about this statement, this ability to transform someone into that teaching role. Another way of saying that is to make them fully human for you. The teacher is the most fully human person.

C4:   I had this situation this week at work, when I had already read this week's assignment. I thought that this would be a moment to stay mindful of the *middah* work that I was doing. It was like a repeat, I have to learn this again and again and again. This is really brilliant. This is about not needing to know everything all the time. If I think I need to hold it together all the time, then I'm setting myself up for failure, arrogance, and all kinds of stuff. This is freedom to say that work or life is partnership, and that other people are holding pieces too, and that asking for help, accepting help, being grateful that others are thinking about this, too. I got in trouble thinking I should know all this.

R: Like almost all of the *middot,* a sort of gut check about whether or not a *middah* is real for you is whether or not it puts you off center. It makes room for someone else on stage. This is very difficult work. *Anavut* pervades all the *middot* because it is about recognizing and honoring the presence of the other, realizing you are not alone.

This is among the most difficult of the *middot,* but it reminds us that this is at work in all the *middot.* There is a kind of *anavut* that operates in all the *middot* we have looked at. Patience, being able to make room for people—all of that is part of this. It almost shouldn't be a single *middah,* but rather recognized as a part of every *middah.* This is extremely difficult because the *yetzer ha-ra* is about us, about me. It has a powerful hold on our souls. This is a real struggle, not just on a superficial level of being proud of what you do, but on a deeper level: being aware that you are not alone in this world and that there is another person that you have a connection to, a space for, at every moment of your life. That is deeply difficult for us, and all of the tools of the *yetzer ha-ra* are out to lead us to rationalization. After all, this is my time, my energy, this person doesn't make any sense . . . all the things we can say to justify our response—caution you that this is not something you will conquer. This is not something that will just go away.

C2:   Something that I heard that struck me, while talking about others being human: "Sometimes we close our hearts and sometimes we open them, but what's really important is to notice whether we are opening or closing." I have been carrying that all week. It's that consciousness of where we are.

R: We call it wakefulness. So that is another way of looking at this, in terms of: When do we go to sleep and when are we really awake? When do we think we're awake when we are really asleep? I think it's okay to summarize it. I think we feel in our bodies a lot earlier than we can think it. In my own life, I can be very conscious of my body saying in the face of this situation that something is going on. Not just tension, but physical movement: Get out of the way of the person! Don't stand face to face, or break contact with someone that would draw me in. It obviously depends on the person and the situation, and there are more profound and less profound examples. In terms of reality, at this point in my life I am much more concerned when I do that with people who I shouldn't be doing it with, rather than people with whom it's not as crucial that I do or don't do it. This is not only about people who annoy us. In many ways, they are easier. But when you are sitting in front of someone who means something to you, and they have something to say and you have the same response—you don't have language to describe the same sort of annoying person. But you know your wife can be an annoying person.

        When we are acting in a role with someone, it most likely is a fear response and is not humility.

C2:   I want to bring in the concept of roles. In this way of thinking about it, role is a reified form of ourselves. We're not there, but we are acting as if we *are* there. People can trigger us to be in a role with body language and tone of voice. We are no longer connected to who we are, but we are going at it with the other person with the same old thing. It's striking that it's connected to humility and to fear. When someone is acting from fear, it's so easy for me to go there myself and act from fear. I was noticing this with a friend. I was talking about my virtues and she was talking abut hers and it got a surreal tone. I thought, "How would I have humility in this situation?"

This is anti-humility.

C3:   The idea is that people don't listen to each other. Transforming the other is a teacher, lots of times we don't listen. For example, this experience in a class: Once I listened to the other person, it was an experience of letting go, thinking about it in terms of that quote. In a way I didn't have a secure sense of myself. I just went out to meet the other but my sense of self was there in the background. I heard and I didn't dissolve. Ultimately the end of this was that I had this strong feeling, I had this sense of all the different parts being part of one mind, different tonalities. It reminded me of what you said about not having to do it all yourself. Lack of humility is thinking you have it and you have to hold onto it. It is not recognizing that these other parts are parts of the whole, and you can learn from them.

R: What makes it even more complicated is that you don't always get any reward. You can't expect the other person to say, "It's been so nice to have you listen to me" or "Gee, now that you've learned from me I want to learn from you." It takes work for you to do what you're doing. The other person may or may not be able to do it; that's irrelevant. It really is about stopping and thinking, thereby taking your mind off the faults. There is nothing in that statement to suggest that the faults are real. Not that you have to convince yourself that there are not faults here. The reality is: just as we have faults so do others, and our role is to manage despite their faults, to learn from them in the face of their faults.

C2:   And one big learning is to learn how to not get hooked, that's the quote. If you don't get hooked, then you're just there.

C3:   The way not to get hooked is to say, "How can I learn from this? What can I learn from them about what they are exhibiting or what it hooks in me?"

R: I want to go back and thank a variety of people who shared quotes. I want to suggest that the quest for quotes is not an insignificant part of this process. Whatever it is you will be looking at in the coming week, if we can build a library of these things, then I think we will be well served. The next piece will be to focus more in the coming months on how to actually make those quotes part of our arsenal. That adds another level of work involved in *middah* work, which is really learning the quotes, having them, making them part of a system, and building a system of self-support—because you are going to be in situations alone, and your response will change not on the basis of intellectual knowledge, but on the basis of tools that you can bring with you.

Through this kind of intense scrutiny of behavior, texts, and Mussar theory, we achieve a level of *hitpa'alut*—that is, a moment of intense spiritual transformation. There are various processes by which we can approach *hitpa'alut,* but the experience itself is momentary. However, this momentary experience translates into specific changes in our behavior, which in turn translate into specific changes of our sense of spiritual connection: through the human other to the Divine Other.

CHAPTER ELEVEN

Worldly Wisdom

One of the basic building blocks of Rav Salanter's Mussar theory is called "worldly wisdom." It refers to two distinct techniques in Mussar theory: one in keeping with the meaning Rav Salanter gave to it, and another an extension of the idea by Rav Simḥa Zissel Braude of Kelm. While all Mussar traditions follow the first, not all follow the second. Since our Mussar theory and practice is strongly influenced by the Elder of Kelm, we include here both techniques.

By "worldly wisdom" Rav Salanter meant acquiring knowledge of how people in the world react to certain emotional and spiritual stimuli. He urged his students to become keen observers of human nature. There were multiple reasons for this interest in human nature. First, in order to help people resist the temptations of the *yetzer ha-ra,* it was important to be able to recognize a range of behaviors and to understand how people rationalized those behaviors. Second, in order to know how to approach different people and convince them to take Mussar seriously, it was necessary to know what "made them tick," so to speak. If, for example, a person was competitive by nature, then presenting Mussar as a competitive activity—setting various goals and equipping those goals with certain trappings of "winning"—might be particularly helpful in enticing that person to explore Mussar. On the other hand, a materialistic person might respond well to an approach explaining how a Mussar sensibility would ultimately help that person's business. Of course, once the person had embarked on a serious Mussar practice these stratagems could be revealed for their being just that. In the meantime, however, they would serve to attract a person who might otherwise not be interested in Mussar.

Rav Simḥa Zissel took Rav Salanter's idea of worldly wisdom one step further. The underlying principle in Rav Salanter's approach was that teaching is a crucial aspect of Mussar, since the practitioner's own Mussar consciousness can be developed further by bringing others to Mussar consciousness. Rav Simḥa extended the scope of this idea: the Mussar teacher must become knowledgeable about the various forms of common knowledge in the surrounding culture (i.e., secular knowledge), since that was the "language" needed to approach many potential Mussar devotees. Since in Simḥa Zissel's day Jews were becoming increasingly interested in Enlightenment ideas and secular education, Rav Simḥa was the first and one of the only Torah teachers to introduce some secular studies at his *yeshiva* in Kelm.

Both of these types of worldly wisdom are relevant to contemporary Mussar practice. In many ways the second (Kelm) definition is superfluous for us. Students coming to Mussar today have a strong grounding in the dominant secular education. To suggest that a successful contemporary spirituality should eschew the importance of this education for an individual's development, as well as for their survival in the culture, would be absurd. However, the Kelm approach takes on heightened significance in our own day, if it allows us to view Mussar as a critique of the ethical shallowness of much of this education, as it is currently delivered in contemporary society. Asking fundamental Mussar questions (such as "How does this aid in bearing the burden of the other?"), even while continuing to pursue the most advanced level of scholarship, does address a pressing concern in the spiritual lives of people today.

At the same time, Rav Salanter's original formulation of worldly wisdom is just as important today as when it was formulated—if not more so. Learning to observe people's behavior and learning how they respond to various stimuli can still be efficacious in judging how to approach them regarding Mussar. Even more importantly, becoming a keen observer of other people's behavior can be an important aid in learning to predict—and then change—one's own behavior.

CHAPTER TWELVE

Mazkeh Ha-Rabbim

azkeh Ha-rabbim literally means "to bring merit to the multitude" and it is used in Mussar theory to refer to the singular importance of teaching Mussar and spreading Mussar consciousness. This was one of the most innovative techniques that Rav Salanter developed in his theoretical structure for transforming Mussar from a literature into a religious practice. He writes in *Ohr Yisrael:*

> We must exhort others to "learn, teach, safeguard, and perform" [quoted from the blessing before the *Shema*] according to the dictates of this wisdom. Only through this can we have good hope for the hereafter, for everyone who is attached to life has faith. If we follow the path of Mussar by working to transform evil to good and extracting the precious metal from the dross, then the Beneficent One will strengthen our hearts. Our sole hope lies in being counted among those who confer merit upon the public, for they, as Pirke Avot (5:18) relates, "shall not be the cause of sin."

This is only one of many passages in which Rav Salanter stresses the importance of spreading Mussar. The benefit of doing so is twofold: it enhances the spiritual well-being of the teacher, the one spreading Mussar, and it also enriches the ones whom he is trying to attract, the potential students. One of Salanter's great insights is that when we are trying to teach and model values for others, we are more likely to act in accord with those values ourselves. Moreover, since the well-being of the other person is the focus of all Mussar practice, actualizing the concern for that well-being by taking responsibility for another's soul directly contributes to my own Mussar consciousness—regardless of how the message is received by the other person.

Mazkeh Ha-rabbim as a contemporary strategy of Mussar practice lies at the outer edge of our concern. Despite the importance that Rav Salanter ascribed to it, this undertaking requires a level of knowledge and *middah* discipline that only the practiced student can achieve. Without humility and patience (two of the *middot* central to *Mazkeh Ha-rabbim*), this enterprise is full of potential pitfalls, requiring us to proceed cautiously. While trying to teach others, it is far too easy to fall into the trap of not seeing the other, and instead imposing ourselves on the other. This would certainly not be spiritually healthy for either them or us.

◱ ◱ ◱

PART FOUR

Mussar and *Mitzvot*

CHAPTER THIRTEEN

Introduction

The Particularity of Love and Choosing Judaism

Jewish life today suffers from a misunderstanding of the nature of—and the urgent necessity of—particularity. We live in a culture that highly values a universalistic perspective and that rewards that perspective both materially and spiritually. The pressure for this universalism is prodigious and can act to quash any leanings we may have toward more particularistic concerns. Some nostalgic loyalty to the various particularities that produce us is permitted and sometimes encouraged, whether these be endogamy, certain cultural institutions, the field of our charitable endeavors, or even the cycle of the family year and celebration of life-cycle events. However, these loyalties are considered entirely expendable under the gaze of universalism. For example, endogamy may wither when we meet someone we love; we may sacrifice to the pressures of our career the cycle of the family year; or we may substitute our personal notions of celebration in place of the requirements of religious law at our life-cycle celebrations. But to privilege universalism in this way is to lose sight of the fact that love is a phenomenon of particularity. Universalism that obliterates particularity runs the risk of cutting itself off from the sources of its own strength. The value of universalism is, indeed, both noteworthy and praiseworthy. It must not, however, precede or obliterate particularity, whose value must also be of paramount concern to us.

Every human being is a particular human being and every command to love is a particular command to love. Every object of our love is a particular person and every neighbor for whom we are responsible is a particular neighbor. If our pleasure from serving each and every one of these particular beloveds does not fully satisfy our desire, that insatiable desire will then become an infinite desire and it will discover an Eternal Beloved. This discovery will only excite a deeper passion in the love for each beloved, but it cannot replace even one such particular beloved.

For Mussar, Jewish particularity is a reflection of the conviction that each of us, as humans, is chosen. We are each the particular agent of an infinite desire. To be a Jew is to be a human being who welcomes the wakefulness of responsibility. Judaism—especially Mussar—offers contemporary Jews a way toward discovering their own humanity. At this level, anyone who manages this discovery is a Jew—or better, the distinction between Jew and non-Jew becomes moot. But as Jews, we believe that there is a mysterious and particularistic love recorded in the Torah, beginning with the Patriarchs and Matriarchs and finding expression in subsequent generations through priests and prophets. This particular love has been the guiding force in shaping our culture, our legacy of Rabbinic Judaism, which is itself a movement obsessively committed to sensitivity to these responsibilities.

Therefore, in the context of contemporary society, the first Mussar act is for a Jew to choose to be a Jew. This must be done not as a rejection of universalism, but as our way toward it. The contemporary Mussar Judaism we are discovering must be a consciously chosen Judaism. For a Jew to adopt the path of Mussar is to prepare for a conversion-like experience.

A central pillar of Mussar ideology is that it does not break any new ground either in theology or in Jewish practice. Rather, it endeavors to programmatically use insights from Torah and tradition to overcome the impediments of human nature and thereby move us from theory to action. For example, like most great Mussar texts, *Mesillat Yesharim (The Path of the Upright)* by Rabbi Moshe Hayyim Luzzatto begins with a disclaimer. The author does not claim that he has anything new to say, but only that what he does have to say has been ignored or relegated to the margins of Jewish study. While Luzzatto predates the Mussar movement, his text is a central one for us.

We are now ready to begin expanding our Mussar concern from the level of personal scrutiny to that of community involvement. By this, we specifically mean involvement in the community out of which Mussar springs and from which it draws its strength. The starting-point of this exploration is a fundamental statement of self-definition of Rabbinic Judaism, found in Pirke Avot:

> Shimon the Righteous was one of the last of the Men of the Great Assembly. He used to say: The world stands on three things: on Torah, on Worship, and on Acts of Saintly Compassion.
>
> *(Avot 1:2)*

This text makes it clear that the tripartite content of Jewish spiritual concern has remained constant: acquiring Torah, worshiping appropriately, and (if we may anticipate Rav Simha) bearing the burden of our fellow. In truth, what are acts of saintly compassion, if not bearing that burden?

We will use this saying of Shimon the Righteous to help structure our description of the fundamentals of Mussar in a contemporary context.

Torah

Torah is the heart of Mussar spirituality. It is a text, a history, an interpretive stance in the world, a call from the Other and a response to another. Its multi-dimensionality serves as an outline to the multi-dimensionality of the contemporary Mussar personality. Let us begin our discussion of Torah by providing some definitions.

The Torah is not a text but a library of texts. It is, of course, the text contained in the *Sefer Torah* (Torah scroll), the Five Books of Moses. It includes, additionally, the rest of the books of the Bible. Taken together, these texts are known as the Written Torah. Understood even more broadly, "Torah" also includes those texts that constitute the Oral Torah. This group is forever fluid. The Mishnah, the Talmud, the midrash, the medieval poets, philosophers and exegetes, and commentators down to our own time—down to this very book—are part of the ongoing conversation about the tradition that is included in our notion of Oral Torah. The vastness of the literature can be daunting. Even to master the variety of languages in which the literature is written can be daunting. However, mastery is not our initial goal. *Acquisition* is our initial goal.

We have already seen in *Ḥokhmah U-Mussar* that acquisition of Torah depends on bearing the burden of another. What is it that we acquire when we acquire Torah? We acquire a thirst for a call or claim upon us. We acquire a desire to be called upon by another and another and another . . . an infinite desire. It is this desire that we bring to the texts of the tradition and that, in turn, we find in the texts of the tradition. That is, we study Torah in order to acquire

Torah. The study of this ancient and venerable literature has always required a motivation. As children, we may have heard simplistic motivations, such as: "Torah will make us better people" or "Torah is the wisdom of our people and will somehow transform us." However, these do not suffice for most contemporary Jews, because we have not really understood the sentences we have heard. "Torah will make us better people" means: the *acquisition* of Torah will make us better people. And becoming better people will, in turn, give us the "eye" with which to learn and study more Torah. All Torah that we will learn will be Oral Torah, since the very act of reading the Written Torah—bringing our own perspective to bear—creates the next layer of Oral Torah. Our motivation is not simply that studying Torah will make us better people. Rather, as people who have accepted the burden of the other, we are now motivated to delve deeper and deeper, to discover additional possibilities for accepting even greater responsibility for others than were discovered by the masters of our tradition in the past.

We thus claim that Torah has a history, and for contemporary Mussar spirituality there can be no blindness, no sleep, in the face of this history. Despite the ancient tradition of delving more and more deeply into the level of responsibility we have for another which is Torah, we know that people were more or less diverted from the true acquisition of Torah in different periods of history. We therefore have a mandate to apply our Mussar sensibility to the accumulated tradition of Torah and to make changes to that tradition that will aid us in better acquiring Torah. Despite the best intentions of many, some crying voices in past ages went unheard. Despite our best intentions, some crying voices in our own time will also go unheard. Only at the messianic horizon would the acquisition of Torah be perfect. And we have learned that any messianic claim of perfection is a false claim. Thus the history of Torah must be part of our contemporary spiritual quest.

For Mussar, the crucial question is always: To what extent does an act or thought better enable us to bear the burden of another? It is this question that is the defining interpretive stance that we take vis-à-vis both the accumulated Torah tradition and the world. Torah is therefore a questioning. Being in the presence of Torah does—and *should*—unsettle our complacencies. It *should* refuse us sleep, since it is a part of the critical Mussar project of wakefulness. Thus, to the extent that we avoid contact with Torah, we allow ourselves to sleep the sleep of the guilty who think they are innocent. Since the Torah comes to us orally, since it is always carried by the human voice that reads it and studies it, it constitutes a voice that calls us from outside and above. In this it is divine, since an infinite voice calls infinitely in every word that has come into being as Torah. The vastness of the literature belies the fact that each word rings with the same voice. The vastness of the literature only emphasizes the vastness of the call and the lengths that we go to when we try to avoid it: staying asleep turns out to be just as much work—if not more—than staying awake. The depth of the call in every word is so compelling, that the attraction of this depth can also militate against the excuse of its vastness that we use to avoid study. There is way too much Torah to study; that is part of its miraculous nature. But every word of Torah yields a world in which to study. Thus contemporary Mussar seekers do not try to study the entirety of the Torah literature. Rather, they savor the world of a single word or phrase: singing it, memorizing it, chanting it, it becomes a part of their consciousness. They learn to live it in every act, and thus are motivated to take on the next word or phrase. The goal is not mastery but acquisition. We acquire Torah by bearing the burden of another, and in the pleasure thereby derived we delve into the text for a word or phrase that will intensify this pleasure. Each phrase thus sought will stimulate the desire to seek another person and to bear yet another burden. What ultimately matters is not how much Torah is learned, but how much Torah is acquired.

The Torah contains a call, and we must respond to that call; the nature and extent of our response will determine how much Torah we learn, or acquire. As we have seen, involvement in the social structures of the community and taking on the yoke of teaching are both acts contingent on the acquisition of Torah. The Mussar student will thus strive to take on more and more of the vastness of the tradition, and then take it out into the world. Despite the difficulty of the literature, Torah-study will thrive when it is undertaken as a response to the call implicit in it. In our own time, the proliferation of texts in translation has, to some degree, eased some of the difficulties associated with text-study, and this is indeed a blessing. We will deal with how to study and what to study in a bit more detail below. But practical questions are irrelevant until we internalize the theoretical question: Why study? Ultimately, we study Torah because the acquisition of Torah consequent on the bearing of the burden of another can transform who we are as human beings.

Avodah

The Hebrew word *avodah* means not only "worship" but also "service" or "work." Certainly worship, as we understand it, includes all of these nuances. True worship, or *avodah,* makes use of all the human arts to express this infinite longing: poetry, music, movement, and art. It is an expression of our infinite desire for the Infinite Beloved, and it is equally an acknowledgment of the burden that we bear on behalf of the Infinite Beloved. *Avodah*/worship can remind us that the Infinite Beloved only interrupts the world we actually live in, through the material needs of the other person who stands in for and carries the trace of the Infinite

Beloved. *Avodah* is also an expression of the effort required for us to remain vigilantly awake to the needs of another. Its regular punctuation of our day, day in and day out, serves to awaken us. It helps us cultivate wakefulness.

Worship as prayer is also an expression of our human cry. Individuals in prayer give voice to their own needs and the community praying together gives voice to the cumulative needs that afflict the entire people, the entire human community. Prayer is an expression of the burden yet to be borne. In this sense, it affirms the reality of the need that is part of the human condition. It affirms, rather than hides, the suffering that is the everyday reality of ordinary people—as well as those horrible moments when ordinary suffering is transformed into extraordinary suffering.

This affirmation of suffering is precisely what recommends regular worship to the contemporary Jew. In our lives, we often create a false veneer under which suffering is hidden or denied. Rather than voicing our pain, we bury it behind a façade of false contentment. Such worship lacks any connection with the reality of the human predicament and can only fall flat. That is not to say that there is nothing else to human life but suffering. It is only to say that even amid our greatest joys we are always aware of our needs, of what we lack, of how we have not reached our goals: of how the very process of living our lives necessarily moves us toward some level of debilitation. To deny this fact obscures even our ability to rejoice.

At the same time, we are painfully aware that prayer will not and does not remove our needs or the suffering we experience. In a certain sense, then, one might say that our prayers are not answered. Yet the answer to prayer cannot simply be the alleviation of our pain, for the alleviation of our pain—of our infinite longing—would require an infinite response, which we have termed messianism. Any claim of messianic fulfillment must be false, for finite beings cannot co-exist with eternity. Messianic fulfillment would end our time and usher in a time about which we cannot speak and in which our concerns would no longer be relevant. Rather, we must look for the answer to our prayers in a different direction. If there is an answer to our prayer, it must be that our own burden should be borne by another. By participating in the community's life of prayer, we effectively make our burden available for others to bear. As we pointed out above, our own suffering is and will always be meaningless as long as it remains individual. However, in a community of prayer our own suffering can potentially give meaning to the others around us who take up our burden and bear it with us. The very act of participating in such a community has a powerful emotional and psychological impact on us. Even when the burden of our suffering is not specifically taken on by another, sharing that burden communally helps give us the feeling of its being borne, and hence the expectation that it someday will be. Prayer provides this hope, even when it can provide nothing else. And it is this hope that will often allow us to carry our own burden a little longer and a little more easily, in anticipation of another's hand reaching out to bear it with us. When this hope washes over us, it prepares the way for an experience of joy—precisely the experience of having the burden borne.

Gemilut Ḥasadim

The term *gemilut ḥasadim* denotes deeds of lovingkindness. Torah and *avodah* are incomplete unless accompanied by action. The acquisition of Torah, leading to our commitment to study, and prayer, expressing the cry of another, both contain the seeds of sleep unless they are actualized in deeds. Both study and prayer can remain on the intellectual level or function as fantasies that make us think we are bearing the burden of another when we are not.

Despite their centrality to Mussar consciousness they are fraught with the dangers of sleep. Only when they are combined with *gemilut hasadim* can we sustain the level of wakefulness we are seeking.

Gemilut hasadim is difficult to render into English literally. The root of the word *gemilut* includes the notion of obligation. It can refer to a loan, a payment, a reward, or even a punishment, when that is the appropriate recompense for a particular act. The root meaning of *hasadim* is kindness and piety. Joining the two words together to create a new term is, obviously, not accidental. Why not simply *hasadim* (or *hesed*), kindness, as the accompaniment to Torah and *avodah?* What is the force of the word *gemilut* in this context and why did the Rabbis choose to use this technical term, rather than expressing their religious consciousness more simply as "Torah, Worship, and Kindness"? Clearly, the inclusion of *gemilut* and the notion of obligation is a recognition of the fact that we are already burdened. We have a debt, something we owe to another, from the very moment we enter consciousness. It is this debt, or our awareness of this debt and our infinite attempt to pay it, which crystallizes the full impact of the tripartite nature of our religious worldview. Acts of kindness cannot be seen simply as acts offered from the goodness of our heart, but must rather be seen in the context of our obligations, as an outgrowth of our relationship to the beloved who stands apart from us, poor and needy and calling.

Everything depends upon *gemilut hasadim*. In fact, the maxim attributed to Shimon the Righteous does not in the end separate the three fields in which human spirituality takes place, but rather unites them. It is the obligatory nature of lovingkindness *(gemilut hasadim)* that undergirds the experience of acquiring Torah, expressing the specific details of our obligations, and facilitates the recognition of our needs and the needs of others that we experience in prayer. *Gemilut hasadim* is not merely about doing good deeds, though they are surely required. Rather, it is about orienting oneself intellectually, spiritually, and practically in the world under the weight of a pre-existing obligation to meet the world with love. Thus, while we can and must separate our experience of the world into discrete phases of experience, a greater unity—a unity of obligation—persists beneath this separation. It is this unity upon which the world stands.

CHAPTER FOURTEEN

Middot and *Mitzvot*

I

The relationship between *middot* (character traits) and *mitzvot* (commandments) is complex. Does the performance of *mitzvot* necessarily inculcate *middot*? Clearly not, since if this were the case, every *mitzvah*-observant Jew would also be a *ba'al middot,* an ethically self-disciplined person. On the one hand, if the goal of *mitzvot* is to produce an ethically self-disciplined person, and if someone can achieve this goal without doing *mitzvot,* then of what intrinsic value are the *mitzvot?* As long as *mitzvot* and *middot* are seen as independent realms, we might wish to privilege one over the other, or to choose one over the other. Given a choice between being ethical and being ritually observant, how should we choose? On the other hand, if we do not feel compelled to bifurcate these notions and make a choice between them, we might assert some degree of dependence—namely, that *mitzvot do* lead to *middot* when performed with the proper *kavanah,* the proper spirit. But if this is the case, why is this spirit so difficult to achieve, and how does one go about achieving it? Moreover, if *mitzvot* require more than just mechanical performance to bring us to ethical self-discipline, if they depend on *kavanah*—which is extrinsic to the *mitzvot* themselves—then does achieving the *middot* via some other route, other than through *mitzvot,* similarly lack some intrinsic power?

These are questions asked by all contemporary Jews. If they are observant Jews, they must ask these questions in order to explain and justify their observance. If they are serious about claiming a Jewish identity without a commitment to observance, they must similarly ask them. And if they are struggling simultaneously with their relationship both to observance and to ethical living, they are most certainly struggling with these questions. These questions can only be ignored by those whose Jewish identity is fully articulated by allegiance to Torah and *mitzvot* without regard for the meaning of those commitments from outside of their insular communities (for example, pre-modern Ḥaredim). Nor are they, strictly speaking, questions limited to the modern period: They are expressed in traditional *ta'amei ha-mitzvot* literature (which endeavors to explain the reasons for the commandments) as well as in Mussar literature, even extending back to the prophetic critique of sacrifices offered without any sense of ethical self-discipline. The pervasiveness of these questions suggests that these concerns are somehow implicit in the very nature of the *mitzvah* system and its inherent tendency for reification—by which we mean confusing instrumentality with its goal, which is in effect idolatry *(avodah zarah).*

To answer these questions, we must begin with theology. However, we must immediately acknowledge that theology for Jews can only be a religious anthropology. We can make no statements that purport to describe the inner workings of God. Rather, we can only describe the intellectual and emotional qualities that describe our experiences of ourselves as quintessentially human. We use these characteristics that describe the quintessence of our humanity as our basic faith statement to describe or reflect our experience of God. We accept, as a matter of faith, that we are created in the image and likeness of God. We stake everything on this assertion and all subsequent theological assertions flow from it. With this in mind, and on the basis of our own experience as well as the record of our experience recorded in Scripture (which, our faith tells us, derives from God's perspective), we identify our choice between good and evil as the very structure of our consciousness of ourselves. We are aware that we are human because at every moment of our existence we are riveted by the need to choose between good and evil. No moment is free of this choice, except for moments when we willfully shrink from the impact of the knowledge that we are human.

The implications of our theology are myriad and complex. But the crucial point is: If the very definition of our consciousness is that we live in the choice between good and evil, then awareness of this choice and its consequences (both for ourselves and also for the world of which we are a part) places a terrible responsibility upon us, since we must not only choose but we must choose the good. Awareness of this terrible responsibility introduces us to our second theological axiom, fear of God—the terror we experience in the face of our obligation to choose between good and evil. This is traditionally called *yirat hashem*. We tremble at the consequences of this imperative to choose. However, in making the choice for good we experience a cessation of fear, actually a pleasure that we come to desire more of. In fact, the more we experience this pleasure, the more we desire it. This desire is the obverse of *yirat hashem;* it is called *ahavat hashem.* Love is an infinite desire that requires an Infinite Beloved—a beloved whom we can never tire of desiring, hence the desire or love of God.

But we have skipped an essential step. Between either *yirat hashem* or *ahavat hashem* and the actual act of choosing between good and evil there lies another dimension that is not infinite, but rather operates very much on the finite—the human—plane. How do we, in fact, learn of the possibility of an infinite desire for an Infinite Beloved? This occurs only after we have exercised our humanity by choosing the good over evil vis-à-vis the other who is not infinite but is close at hand, the other whose good gives us the pleasure that will ultimately excite in us an infinite desire for pleasure from an Infinite Beloved. Our first theological axiom was that we are created in the image and likeness of God, and must therefore choose between good and evil. Our second theological axiom was that this responsibility raises terror *(yirah)* within us, along with the possibility of pleasure *(ahavah)* we receive from choosing the good. Our third theological axiom, then, is that we must choose the good of our neighbor. This principle reaches us in the language of scriptural commandment: *ve-ahavta le-rayakha kamokha,* "You shall love your neighbor as yourself" (Leviticus 19:18).

Our human consciousness derives from the tension between good *(yetzer ha-tov)* and evil *(yetzer ha-ra)* and precipitates in us both terror *(yirah)* and the possibility of love *(ahavah)*. When we analyze the actions by which both *yirah* and *ahavah* are actualized in life, we discover the *middot*—that is, the qualities of character that determine our ability to act in the world in response to *yirah* and *ahavah*. These traits include: orderliness, patience, equanimity, humility, kindness, etc. However, the sphere in which our mastery of these traits is tested is that of our interactions with our neighbor. How our humility impacts us is of some interest, of course. But how it impacts our neighbor is the point at which a command, or *mitzvah,* comes into being. It is in regard to our neighbor that we locate the interface between *middot* and *mitzvot*.

At this point of interface, we must continue to think theologically a bit longer before returning to the practical discussion of the relationship between *middot* and *mitzvot*. The first question we must now attempt to answer is: Who is our neighbor, and how do we get from the finitude of our neighbor to the infinite desire that describes the love of God? The second question we must address is: How do we get from the central commandment of *ve-ahavta le-rayakha kamokha* to the detailed system of *mitzvot* that characterizes Judaism?

The answer to the first question is straightforward: Our neighbor is that person who, being created in the image and likeness of God, embodies that which we can experience of God in the finite dimension. My neighbor is not God, but serving my neighbor is as close as I can come to serving God in this world. My neighbor's closeness to me is not incidental. It is by virtue of this closeness that I am originally brought from mere material existence to human consciousness. That is, my first neighbor is the one who has cared for me, answered my cry in the night, and awakened in me the desire that will eventually move outward, to care for that neighbor and, ultimately, for others to whom I will be close. The neighbor may be my parents and my teachers. And since my loving service for them will not satisfy my desire, I will expand my care to include another and another in that love—until it will indeed require an Infinite Beloved as the object of my love.

To answer the second question we will use the word wakefulness, which we treat as a theological term. We assert that our consciousness threatens to shut down when confronted by the terror *(yirah)* resulting from our obligation to choose the good of our neighbor as we would choose the good for ourselves—or even before ourselves or (in the ideal or messianic world) instead of ourselves. To put it simply, we go to sleep. The system of *mitzvot* articulated in the Torah and developed further by later Jewish tradition is intended to do two things. *Mitzvot* keep us awake to our previously understood obligations. Moreover, they allow us to invoke the community to share the burden that existentially would otherwise be all our own. It may seem impossible for me to meet all of my obligations to increasing numbers of neighbors to whom

I am near. However, the community may be able, through just laws, to care for them appropriately.

It is clear from these considerations that *middot* are prerequisite to *mitzvot* and that *mitzvot* are instrumental in actualizing *middot*. It should also be clear that *middot* can act as a critique of *mitzvot* and that *mitzvot,* particularly in their communal application, can act as a critique of the individualism implicit in *middot*. Thus, the answers to our earlier questions are also clear, though not simple. Certainly there is a direct correspondence between doing *mitzvot* and inculcating *middot,* but it is a reciprocal and mutually reinforcing relationship. Each impacts the other; each is necessary for the full articulation of the other. The correspondence between *middot* and *mitzvot* reflects a deeper relationship between the two terms in a larger theological context. To examine this broader context, including a larger complex of theological terms, we will now turn to Psalm 19 to further explore the relationship between these two terms and others.

Psalm 19:2–14

verse 2:   The heavens declare the glory of God, the sky proclaims His handiwork.

verse 3:   Day to day makes utterance, night to night speaks out.

verse 4:   There is no utterance, there are no words, whose sound goes unheard.

verse 5:   Their voice carries throughout the earth, their words to the end of the world. He placed in them a tent for the sun,

verse 6:   who is like a groom coming forth from the chamber, like a hero, eager to run his course.

verse 7:   His rising-place is at one end of heaven, and his circuit reaches the other; nothing escapes his heat.

verse 8:   The teaching of the LORD is perfect, renewing life; the decrees of the LORD are enduring, making the simple wise;

verse 9:   The precepts of the LORD are just, rejoicing the heart; the instruction of the LORD is lucid, making the eyes light up.

verse 10: The fear of the LORD is pure, abiding forever; the judgments of the LORD are true, righteous altogether, *verse 11:* more desirable than gold, than much fine gold; sweeter than honey, than drippings of the comb.

verse 12: Your servant pays them heed; in obeying them there is much reward.

verse 13: Who can be aware of errors? Clear me of unperceived guilt,

verse 14: and from willful sins keep Your servant; let them not dominate me; then shall I be blameless and clear of grave offense.

Psalm 19 divides the cosmos into three sections. At the top of the map are the heavens (verses 2–7). At the bottom of the map is chaos, the world bereft of either *middot* or *mitzvot* (verses 13–14, which speak of *shegi'ot, zeidim, and pesha*—errors, sins, and transgressions). Between the two is the human world (verses 8–12). At the border between the world of chaos and the world of people we find, indeed, the first mention of a person in this psalm: *ovdekha,* "Your servant." This is indeed where we find ourselves: at the border between the world above and the world that results from our choice for evil. At this border we find the Torah of God (verse 8). Torah is above us on this map, between us (far down in verse 12) and the heavens (looking upward, beginning in verse 7). What is between this exalted Torah and us? In ascending order, from the point at which we find ourselves choosing to avoid the evil described below us on the map, we find: *mishpetei Adonai* (ordinances of Adonai), *yirat Adonai* (fear of Adonai), *mitzvot Adonai* (commandments of Adonai), *pikkudei Adonai* (judgments of Adonai), *eidut Adonai* (testimony of Adonai), and finally *torat Adonai* (the Torah of Adonai) far above us at the border of the heavens. Thus in the domain of the cosmos that we occupy, just above the chaos of sin, we find law. In Psalm 19 this probably does not refer to *mitzvot* per se, but rather to natural or common-sense law that—barely!—separates human society from utter chaos. And above that we find *yirah.* The consciousness of our obligation to a world of goodness begins above natural law but below *mitzvot* (which are themselves below judgments and testimony, which are ethical categories). Only then, after reaching *yirah,* do we ascend to Torah. Thus there is a correspondence between *middot* and *mitzvot.* Through this correspondence, they both together point to a level of spiritual power above either one. Ascending to this level of spiritual power should become the joint quest of our *mitzvah-*observant community and *middah-*conscious community, transforming them along the way into one community.

CHAPTER FIFTEEN

Staying Awake and Sharing the Burden through *Halakhah*

Jews are wont to define their relationship to Judaism in terms of specific acts, both ritual and ethical. Regardless of one's level of observance, one measures one's Judaism in terms of one's relationship to these acts, this set of behaviors and regulations that the tradition calls *halakhah*. The distinctions among the contemporary denominations of Judaism are sometimes claimed to be rooted in philosophical or theological distinctions, but more commonly they are seen as growing from different approaches to *halakhah*. Although halakhic differences can and do point to underlying theological and philosophical differences, these ideological differences are more readily grasped when viewed through their actualization in *halakhah*.

The Mussar approach to *halakhah* depends on the theory we have already outlined. Theologically speaking, the purported divine nature of *halakhah* can be determined only by recourse to our experience. And that experience, which determines our understanding of the divine nature of *halakhah,* is our experience of the world that leads us to the obligation of wakefulness. It is only through the compelling burden of wakefulness that any intimation of the divine via-a-vis *halakhah* makes sense. Therefore, if *halakhah* is to have any authority or hold over us, then it must by its very nature carry this compelling wakefulness with and for us.

Halakhah is the vehicle by which the divine makes its way into our experience, as the burden we carry for another—even as we are unable to understand its nature through reason. *Halakhah* is the concretization of love, the source of our striving for that which gives us pleasure, the path on which we walk in order to remain vigilantly awake to the needs of another. It is also how we share the burden of this wakefulness with a community for as long as we are unable to bear it alone. *Halakhah* is our lifeline in a world still awaiting the messianic era. Since the wakefulness we have described is a consequence of our infinite desire for an Infinite Beloved, we thus understand *halakhah* to be the expression of that infinite desire for the Infinite Beloved. The divine aspect of *halakhah* is contained in the direction or path on which it guides us. And that is, of course, the literal meaning of the word *halakhah.*

Halakhah, the traditional system of prescribed and forbidden behaviors, is the Jewish way of keeping us awake in our infinite desire for the Infinite Beloved. This involves a thorough review of our behavior, focusing both on desirable actions that we need to foster and harmful actions that we need to avoid. The *halakhah* is a physical expression of the response of those who came before us in their attempt to bear the burden of another, and another, and the Other, throughout history. Therefore, *halakhah* has a history, and it is not simply synonymous with Torah. We have already seen that Torah is what we acquire as a consequence of bearing the burden of another; its text tradition speaks to the undertaking of that burden in a contemplative mode. *Halakhah* emerges from the contemplation of Torah. It is based on Torah, but it is equally based on *avodah* (worship) and *gemilut ḥasadim*. These three pillars of the world, which we have already described, always undergird and anchor the *halakhah*. Insofar as *halakhah* is based on Torah, the shape of the acts it requires is determined by Jewish experience. Insofar as *halakhah* is based on *avodah,* the shape of its acts is determined by the voice of those who suffer and cry out. Insofar as *halakhah* is based on *gemilut ḥasadim,* the shape of its acts is determined by the imperative to respond to another's suffering. *Halakhah,* therefore, cannot be subdivided or compartmentalized: it cannot be adequately described by a division into ethics and rituals (or any other categories, for that matter). It is a whole cloth constantly being woven, un-woven, and re-woven, depending on the circumstances. This is the radical stance of Mussar toward *halakhah* and it is the reason that the Mussar movement was disdained by established Jewish authority in its time. Even in our own time, established Jewish authority will continue to scorn a contemporary Mussar, since establishment authorities have a vested interest in maintaining the status quo. But the status quo undermines the insistence of our infinite desire for the Infinite Beloved.

We have tried to define a Mussar approach to *halakhah,* although a full review of halakhic norms from a Mussar perspective is beyond the scope of this project. However, we will deal below with a few major areas of halakhic concern. We hope, thereby, to give examples of the application of this Mussar perspective, with reference to a few practical halakhic matters. Specifically, we will use a contemporary Mussar analysis to deal with prayer (in the practical sense of liturgy), observance of the Sabbath and Festivals, and the study of Torah.

CHAPTER SIXTEEN

Hearing the Cry
and Giving It Voice

P rayer is a very important part of the Mussar approach to Jewish life. Prayer serves to express in human terms our infinite desire for the Infinite Beloved, and also to give voice to the cry of the suffering of another so that their cry might elicit our response. But this describes prayer in the broadest sense; the question of statutory prayer, the regular halakhic discipline of thrice-daily prayer, needs further elucidation. In addition, the actual content of the liturgy (the fixed Jewish prayer texts) needs to be explored. Finally, we must consider the possibility of generating new prayers, both individual and communal, in light of both our commitment to a Mussar sensibility and the contemporary context of our prayer services. This will not only address the subject of prayer in particular, but will also allow us more generally to explore the *halakhah* of prayer, as an example of a contemporary Mussar approach to *halakhah*. This is potentially a vast undertaking and cannot be explored fully here. But we hope that this brief exposition will serve as a beginning of this important work, which others will continue.

The *halakhah* requires that every obligated Jew recite three daily prayer services. Traditionally, this meant Jewish males over the age of thirteen. Contemporary liberal Jews for whom the idea of religious obligation is still meaningful have expanded this definition of obligation to include women as well. Indeed, a Mussar spirituality demands this expansion of the idea of obligation, precisely because wakefulness itself is an obligation incumbent on every human being. Since disciplined prayer helps inculcate wakefulness, it should likewise be viewed as an obligation for all people. Men and women are equal in their humanity, and so they are equal in the possibility of developing an infinite desire for an Infinite Beloved. They are equally susceptible to what we've called sleep, and prayer functions equally in encouraging wakefulness for both genders.

Both the obligatory nature of prayer and its insistence in our lives—that it must be recited three times a day, wherever we are and whatever we are doing, and, most importantly, whatever our mood—are expressions of the highest Mussar sensibility. But moving beyond the formal requirements of prayer, what can we say about the *content* of the prayers? How do they contribute to either wakefulness or infinite desire? We will here focus on the content of the morning prayer service, *Shaḥarit*.

The traditional *Shaḥarit* service is comprised of up to four independent liturgical units, each of which has a separate history and function in the service as a whole:

1. *Birkot Ha-shaḥar*—the morning blessings (the preliminary service)
2. *Pesukei D'zimra*—verses of song (additional introductory prayers)
3. *Shaḥarit*—the statutory morning prayers (the core of the service)
4. *Keriat Ha-torah*—the reading of the Torah (part of the service on Mondays and Thursdays, as well as on Shabbat and Festivals)

On Sabbaths and Festivals, the morning prayer service is rounded out by *Musaf,* an additional prayer service.

Birkot Ha-shaḥar consists of prayers and blessings that were originally recited at home upon awakening. They recognize the danger of sleep and the glory of wakefulness, in both the physical and spiritual senses. This section also contains sections of the Written Torah and Oral Torah so that, upon recognizing the joy of wakefulness, we might immediately engage in contemplative Torah study. With sleep banished, we are able to recommence our bearing the burden of others. This recognition attaches us to Torah, which in turn motivates our study.

Pesukei D'zimra consists almost entirely of selections from the Book of Psalms and is intended to fulfill the rabbinic advice that one should not enter into serious prayer until one has put one's soul into the appropriate spirit. Formally these sections focus on God's role as Creator of the universe. The philosophic implication of creation is that we are not responsible for our own being, and this fact impresses upon us the gift that we owe the other for our lives and the ensuing obligation that we have to bear the burden of the other. In that way these selections primarily deal with the dependence of human beings on the other and the joy that comes from both having one's own burden borne and bearing the burden of another.

We have dealt only in passing with these two essentially non-statutory parts of the morning liturgy. They represent the tendency of Jewish liturgy to grow and to reiterate themes implicit in the statutory liturgy. We now turn our attention to the *Shaḥarit* service proper, which is the oldest section of the liturgy and best expresses the theological ideas that the Rabbis wished to articulate in the liturgy. The *Shaḥarit* service consists of two basic units of liturgy: (1) *Keriat Shema* and (2) the *Amidah*. The *Shema* is a selection of biblical passages, certainly one of the best known among Jews throughout the ages. Since reciting the *Keriat Shema* is a *mitzvah*—that is, its recitation is obligatory—it is both preceded and followed by *berakhot* (blessings), which acknowledge the imperative that we are either about to fulfill or have just fulfilled. *Keriat Shema* in the morning is preceded by two blessings and followed by one. The content of these blessings is not unimportant, as the *berakhot* direct our attention to what the Rabbis believed was being affirmed by reciting the *Shema*.

The first blessing before the *Shema* addresses the universal nature of God as Creator. While it is a long blessing, the concluding lines will give us a good sense of its focus:

> To praiseworthy God they sweetly sing;
> in song they celebrate the living, enduring God.
> For God is unique, doing mighty deeds, creating new life,
> championing justice, sowing righteousness,
> reaping victory, bringing healing.
> Awesome in praise, Sovereign of wonders,
> God, in His goodness, renews Creation day after day.
> So sang the psalmist: "Praise the Creator of great lights,
> for God's love endures forever."
> Cause a new light to illumine Zion.
> May we all soon share a portion of its radiance.
> Praised are You, Adonai, Creator of lights.

> *(Siddur Sim Shalom)*

This blessing celebrates the physical world and the love implicit in God's gift of the physical world to human beings. In a sense, nature is the first to bear the burden of human beings, since we are ultimately dependent on the cycles of nature. Nature, therefore, might be understood as the first "caretaker" to whom we as humans are obligated. In turn, the primacy of our obligation to nature reminds us that the first burden that we are obligated to bear toward another is also the "natural" (i.e., physical) burden. Whether or not others have food, clothing, and other material necessities precedes any consideration of other obligations we might have toward them.

When we praise the God of the natural universe, we are praising God for allowing our burden as creatures to be borne, and also for allowing us—together with God—to bear those burdens for others. We will return to these ideas below, as we explicate the *Shema* itself.

The second blessing before the *Shema* has a very different theme.

> Deep is Your love for us, Adonai our God,
> boundless Your tender compassion.
> *Avinu Malkenu,* You taught our ancestors life-giving laws.
> They trusted in You:
> for their sake graciously teach us.
> Our Maker, merciful Provider, show us mercy:
> grant us discernment and understanding.
> Then will we study Your Torah, heed its words,
> teach its precepts, and follow its instructions,
> lovingly fulfilling all its teachings.
>
> Open our eyes to Your Torah;
> help our hearts cleave to Your *mitzvot.*
> Unite all our thoughts to love and revere You.
> Then we will never be brought to shame,
> for we trust in Your awesome holiness,
> and will delight in Your deliverance.
> Bring us safely from the four corners of the earth,
> and lead us in dignity to our holy land,
> for You are the Source of deliverance.
> You have called us from all peoples and tongues,
> constantly drawing us nearer to You,
> that we may lovingly offer You praise,
> proclaiming Your Oneness.
> Praised are You, Adonai, who loves the people Israel.

> *(Siddur Sim Shalom)*

In this blessing we acknowledge the particular relationship between God and Israel, recognizing our election and the love that is implicit in this election. This is a key element in the construction of a theology of Jewish prayer. We have already dealt both with the notion of particularity in relationship to love and also with the notion of election, and these are key issues in Mussar spirituality. We accept upon ourselves the burden of this love just as we are poised to give voice to the cry of those who suffer and express an infinite desire for an Infinite Beloved. It is at this moment that we fully recognize that love *is* this burden. Again, we will develop the connections between these introductory blessings and the content of the prayers that follow in our comments on the *Shema* itself.

The power of the three paragraphs of the *Shema* rests, in large part, on the fact that we are not speaking. We are, in a way, re-speaking—or, more accurately yet, God is speaking to us and through us. It is a re-enactment of revelation itself. In a very real sense we are doing exactly what our ancestors did when they (and we) stood at Sinai. We are opening our mouths and the words of God are issuing forth from us. Then, as now, our question is only: What do these words mean?

> Hear, O Israel: Adonai is our God, One God.
>
> *(author's translation)*

First, the word *shema* (hear): God's words require our attention. God calls and we must hear. The ongoing nature of this call is presupposed by our daily experience of it. When we listen, God is speaking through us. In truth, listening requires a little silence. When we are constantly talking there is no room for God's word in our mouths. In fact, the word *shema* is used elsewhere in the Torah in exactly that way, to command the silence necessary to hear the divine voice. In Deuteronomy we find the phrase: "Listen and be silent" (27:9). In a world where everyone is always talking, we can neither listen to nor speak in God's voice.

Second, the word *yisrael:* God is talking to and through

Israel—not through any one individual or even through Moses, but through the *entire* nation of Israel. Thus, we have to listen to each other because God is speaking through each of us in community. This is difficult to do. Perhaps even more difficult than listening or being silent, it is difficult to recognize the voice of God issuing from our neighbor. And if we accept the interpretation of Rav Simha Zissel that the word *yisrael* here really means *all* people, then the task becomes even more difficult.

Third, the words *Adonai, Eloheinu, Adonai.* The God speaking to us and through us does not stand still. Sometimes God is *Adonai,* the God of the Tetragrammaton, the God of *yod, hei, vav, hei.* This is the God that we can name but cannot grasp, the God who passes in and out of our lives. Sometimes, however, God is *Eloheinu,* our God, the God of prayer, the God of ritual, the God of judgment, law, and society. Then, sometimes, that God disappears and *Adonai* returns. God does not remain static and the God we need to help us build communities is always challenging us by breaking out of the bounds we set within those communities.

Finally, the word *ehad.* Even though God does not stand still, God is nevertheless One. The God speaking through me, speaking through you, bound in the laws of the community, escaping the laws of community and soaring out into the worlds beyond the world—all these perceptions are the result of our own fragmentation. God, however, is whole, is One. This oneness is at the heart of the *Shema* and at the heart of Jewish tradition. It is at the heart of the re-enactment of revelation, which in Jewish tradition conveys a content. That content is found in the first paragraph of the *Shema,* the *V'ahavta,* and it is comprised of three themes: love, teaching, and remembering. God's words in the *Shema* outline the system of navigating the world so that we can get from reciting the *Shema* to reciting the *Shema* without forgetting it, without allowing ourselves to go to sleep.

The first paragraph of the *Shema,* called the *V'ahavta,* states:

> You shall love Adonai your God with all your heart, with all your soul, with all your might. And these words, which I command you this day, you shall take to heart. Teach them, diligently, to your children, and recite them at home and away, night and day. Bind them as a sign upon your hand, and as a reminder above your eyes. Inscribe them upon the doorposts of your homes and upon your gates.

(Siddur Sim Shalom)

In discussing the content of the *V'ahavta,* we will begin with love. Love is the primary response expected of us following this re-enactment of revelation, just as it was the primary response expected of us after the initial revelation at Sinai. By the very force of the experience of God's speaking through us in love, we are commanded to love—to love God. But God, we have just learned, never stands still. How can we love a moving force? The answer must be: by concentrating on the essence of that moving force as best we can. If God speaks through the voices of the people around us, then we must show our love for God by listening to those around us. If others are indeed speaking with God's voice, they are saying: *love me—with all your heart, with all your soul, with all your might.* Through the heart we hear the cry of others. Through the soul we connect this cry with the cry of God. "All our might," the Rabbis taught, refers to material sustenance. When we hear our neighbor's cry and recognize in it the cry of God, we are commanded to support it, to take care of it, to bear its burden. This must be done not only with our words, but with all of our material resources.

The unity that commands this love cannot be part time. Nor can it be limited to one person or to one generation. The love that revelation occasions requires teaching. This is done most effectively by ourselves being enwrapped in the love we've experienced, at all times: at home, while out walking, while waking up and going back to sleep. This is love that is expressed by real people living real lives. But because we are real people living real lives, we will forget and we will fall back to sleep. So we must endeavor to remind ourselves of this love. Daily we wrap these words around ourselves as reminders; daily we see them posted on our doorways. However, they are not there simply to be worn or to be kissed. We fulfill the words of the *Shema* only when the presence of the symbols actually reminds us to love, to strengthen our wakefulness. It is not accidental that our tradition chose to understand these particular words of the *Shema* as *the* words that we are to carry with us at all times. In them, the purpose and message of the rest of the Torah become clear: to love, to teach, and to remember.

The themes of the *Shema* are interwoven. One cannot really speak of teaching without love, or of love without teaching, nor of either without remembrance. The second paragraph, however, treats the second content area, teaching, in more detail:

> If you will earnestly heed the *mitzvot* I give you this day, to love Adonai your God and to serve God with all your heart and all your soul, then I will favor your land with rain at the proper season, in autumn and in spring, and you will have an ample harvest of grain, wine, and oil. I will assure abundance in the fields for your cattle. You will eat to contentment. Take care lest you be tempted to stray, and to worship false gods. For then Adonai's wrath will be directed against you. God will close the heavens and hold back the rains; the earth will not yield its produce. You will soon disappear from the good land which Adonai is giving you. Therefore, impress these words of Mine upon your heart. Bind them as a sign upon your hand; let them be a reminder above your eyes. Teach them to your children. Repeat them at home and away, night and day. Inscribe them upon the doorposts of your homes and upon your gates. Then your days and the days of your children, on the land that Adonai swore to give to your ancestors, will endure as the days of the heavens over the earth.

> *(Siddur Sim Shalom)*

The opening line of the paragraph enunciates the goal of teaching: to listen and to love, for there are consequences attached to both. Teaching thus has cosmic importance, since its goal is tied to the very structure of the universe. The teaching spoken of here is not utilitarian in the sense of learning in order to control the world. Rather, it is learning in order to answer the question, "Why am I here?" The content of the *Shema* is not just a matter of good advice and we cannot simply choose whether or not to accept its doctrine. It makes a powerful claim on us: that there is a teaching whose source is divine and that takes the form of commandments, and its imperative is obedience in love. The "in love" part is not incidental, but rather is crucial. Our obedience to the commands is predicated on our experience of love. We are told to listen to God and hear the commandments, and to love. What is the relationship between commandment and love? True obedience, the only obedience that meaningfully compels a person, is that obedience assumed in response to loving another. Whatever we do for our children, our spouse, our parents, or our good friends, we do out of love. Love compels us to respond to their needs. Thus our compulsion to do God's will, so to speak, can only be forged in love. Any other type of obedience is born of oppression.

The obedience to God born of love, like the obedience we give others out of love, has consequences. We are told that if we serve God with all our heart and soul we will receive a reward. The rain will fall at its proper time and the grain and grass will be plentiful. We are also told that if we are not careful, if we turn aside from this obedience, we will incite God to anger and all of the promises of reward will turn into promises of punishment. Viewed from the point of view of temporal power, of state oppression, these words seem distasteful. But these are not words of a temporal power or of a state. Rather, they are an analysis of the consequences of love and, as such, they must ring true in our ears. Our obedience results from the realization of the obligations love places upon us. When we understand this, we also understand that betraying that love, turning away from meeting our responsibilities to that love, has real consequences. Those consequences exist in the everyday world, and they may be as dire as the cessation of the rain or the failure of the harvest. They make it either possible or impossible to live.

How do these words, which are founded on an experience of love, transcend the limits of a language that sounds like the threats of a despot? How can I recite these words of threat and counterthreat without feeling that I am being coerced, but instead feel them as the natural outpouring of my own response to a lover? In other words, how can we experience God's love so that our obedience becomes a given? The answer is: by reciting this prayer. If we return to the premise of the *Shema*—that we are not speaking, but that God is speaking through us and to us—then we can understand the crucial mechanism that the prayer employs. When we keep silent but listen and recite these words, we can then become the vehicle for God's revelation, as we speak the words in exactly the same way that the people of Israel spoke them (or heard them) on Sinai. And Sinai is considered the crowning moment of God's love for Israel. It was then that God, as an act of compassion, revealed the gift of Torah. We do not remember Sinai; we experience it. We were there and we are there again. We respond with love to the majesty of this moment of revelation. To live in a world loved by God requires us to take on God's obligation for caring for this world and thereby for God. In other words, we become deeply cognizant of our obligations, of our responsibilities in the world. We are overcome by this overwhelming need to obey, coming from deep within ourselves and not from some outside force or oppressor. We threw off such outside forces long ago, at the Red Sea. Now we respond not in fear but out of love.

Now that we have experienced God's love, the burst of God's

voice issuing out of our own mouths, we can act in response to this love. We can more powerfully reiterate the need to communicate this experience to ourselves and to others. We have a need to bind this experience to our hearts and to bind the words to our arms and between our eyes, so that we will not avoid them. Most importantly of all, we must teach them to our children. We now understand that this means to give to our children the opportunity to say these words over and over again, until the words of God are speaking to them and through them.

Whereas the second paragraph of the *Shema* describes the complex relationship of love, obedience, and teaching, the third paragraph is concerned primarily with the role of memory. It is also concerned with the role of ritual, which is at once concrete and symbolic, and also with the movement from ritual to redemption:

> Adonai said to Moses: Instruct the people Israel that in every generation they shall put *tzitzit* on the corners of their garments and bind a thread of blue to the *tzitzit*. Look upon these *tzitzit* and you will be reminded of all the *mitzvot* of Adonai and fulfill them, and not be seduced by your heart nor led astray by your eyes. Then you will remember and observe all My *mitzvot* and be holy before your God. I am Adonai your God who brought you out of the land of Egypt to be your God. I, Adonai, am your God.

> *(Siddur Sim Shalom)*

This third paragraph is neatly divided into two very distinct parts: the first deals with the ritual of *tzitzit* (fringes) and the second deals with memory. The section on memory is further subdivided into a section calling for memory of the commandments and a section proclaiming God as the redeeming God. We will follow these divisions, to explain the paragraph itself and also to understand its role within the *Shema* as a whole.

We begin, therefore, with the *mitzvah* of *tzizit*. Israel is commanded to affix fringes to the corners of their garments, with each fringe containing a thread of blue. The theme of teaching, which is introduced in the first paragraph of the *Shema* and further developed in the second paragraph, is continued here. While the second paragraph focuses on God's great teaching, to listen and to love, the third paragraph is concerned with sustaining that teaching. It locates in the sensory world the vulnerability that human beings must possess and from which they must also be protected. If the *Shema* is concerned in its opening and first paragraph with hearing, with attentive listening, and with quieting ourselves to hear so that the divine voice can speak to us and through us, then this closing paragraph is concerned with seeing. That is a concern with living in the world of noise, a world often too noisy to allow us to continue to hear the voice we once heard. Amid the noise and the deafening it produces we must rely on our sight. We must trust our eyes to convey what our ears can no longer hear. But our eyes can be so easily deceived and they can be so easily closed in slumber, so that the instrument of our salvation can also become the instrument of our downfall. Our eyes are the conduit to and from our hearts, and so the love flowing into and out of our hearts can become diverted by the lusts of the world, which are taken in through our eyes. We cannot completely block out the noise of the world, but we can purify our view of it by looking at the fringes and their thread of blue. Why is blue prescribed? Because it is the color of the sky. Moreover, blue—deep, clear, sapphire blue—is the color of the pavement beneath the throne of God, through which God views the world. This is described in *Parashat Mishpatim* (Exodus 24), and this same view was also described in some detail in *Ḥokhmah U-Mussar*. Blue thus reminds us to view the world from the perspective of God. Rav Simḥa Zissel taught us that God's view of creation is made up of the suffering of humanity. This view of the world is replicated by performing the commandments. That is why and what we must remember, and it is this view that bridges the gap between the first and second sections of this paragraph. When we view the world from God's perspective we are brought into contact with the very meaning of redemption, and the aim of our liturgy is to bring about that redemption. This theme of redemption, of seeing the world through God's eyes instead of through our own human eyes, takes us back to the opening of the *Shema* and its call to listen, and at the same time takes us forward to the blessing after the *Shema* and to the *Amidah,* a complex part of the liturgy whose grand theme is precisely the Jewish vision of redemption.

The *berakhah* after the *Shema,* called *Emet Ve-yatziv,* is long and complex. Both its length and its complexity are warranted, as it functions to connect the two central liturgical acts of Jewish worship: recitation of the *Shema* and recitation of the *Amidah.* We have already identified the major themes of the *Shema* as teaching, love, obedience, and redemption, and we have learned that, according to the third paragraph of the *Shema,* redemption means seeing the world through the eyes of God. The key to understanding this *berakhah* after the *Shema* lies in anticipating the function of the *Amidah,* which follows it. At this point, then, we must digress slightly in order to discuss a few fundamental ideas about the *Amidah,* to which we will return later on. This is, however, necessary here in order to explicate *Emet Ve-yatziv.*

The *Amidah* is the liturgical replacement for the sacrifices that were offered in the Temple in Jerusalem. We recite the *Amidah* whenever a sacrifice would have been offered, during the period that the Temple was in existence. The act of sacrifice is complex and may be interpreted in many different ways. For our purposes, we will focus on sacrifice as an act in which human beings confronted the inevitability of death, the inevitability of a human experience that God, who cannot die, does not experience. Sacrifice was an attempt to find meaning in this ultimately lonely and inevitable erasure of our consciousness, by sharing the moment with God. God's acceptance of the offering represents a straining of the divine imagination to include death, vicariously, in the experience of God. Through God's gracious acceptance of this moment of ultimate human solitude, human solitude is overcome—and death and the fear of death are likewise transcended. This loneliness of death can be abolished forever, suggests the religious imagination, when people will see the world through God's eyes, caring for other human beings with the caring of God in our hearts. The act of sacrifice is potentially redemptive, because it can trigger an intimation of what it would be like to live in a world in which redemption can be maintained. This was the world of sacrifices, and the world of the *Amidah* attempts to replicate this world. We will explore below how successful it is in this regard. However, being aware of these themes of the *Amidah* now allows us to turn back to the *berakhah* following the *Shema*. Through this *berakhah,* we come to the *Amidah* already redeemed. To believe that we are already redeemed—that we do, in fact, see the world through God's eyes and therefore are ready to extend this redemption into eternity through the act of sacrificial sharing with God—requires an extraordinary imaginative affirmation, an act better known as faith.

And that is where our *berakhah* begins, with as strong an affirmation of faith as one could possibly make in mere language:

> True and firm *(emet ve-yatziv),* right and faithful, beloved and precious, good and beautiful is this Your teaching unto us forever and ever.
>
> As for our ancestors, so too for our descendants: Your teaching is good and endures forever and ever. It is a truth, a faith, a law that shall not pass away.
>
> It is true that You are Adonai our God and the God of our ancestors, our Ruler and our ancestors' Ruler, our Redeemer and the Redeemer of our ancestors.

> *(author's translation)*

We affirm our faith in God's teaching and the result of that teaching, redemption. We affirm it as a fact of the past that incorporates the present. Because our ancestors were redeemed, we too are redeemed. Because our ancestors were the recipients of God's love, that love engulfs us as well. As our ancestors responded to this act of love with song, so do we, too, memorialize our redemption in verse, celebrating not only God's love but also the vision that act of love has given us, the vision of the world from God's perspective:

> Happy is the person who hears Your commandments, Your Torah,
>   and puts Your words upon their heart.
> You bring low the haughty and raise up the lowly;
> You lead forth the captives and deliver the meek.
> You help the poor,
> and answer Your people when they call unto You.

> *(Siddur Sim Shalom)*

This is what it means to be redeemed from Egypt: to see the world from God's perspective and to realize that one is already redeemed, by virtue of this "seeing." And when we remember that we are redeemed, we can join our voices again, in another act of sublime religious imagination, with the people of Israel at the Red Sea in the moment of their realization of redemption. We sing an ancient song, which the liturgy nevertheless calls a "new song." It is both: although ancient, the song is always new when we sing it:

> Who is like You, Adonai, among the mighty?
> Who is like unto You, glorious in holiness,
> Revered in praises, doing wonders?
> Singing a new song, they proclaimed Your sovereignty:
> "Adonai shall reign for ever and ever."

> *(Siddur Sim Shalom)*

Thus, the extraordinary liturgical unit known as *Keriat Shema* or *Shema U-virkhotehah* (the Recitation of the *Shema,* or the *Shema* and Its Blessings) comes to a conclusion amid this crescendo. We have progressed through several theological steps: beginning with our almost naive celebration of the God of nature in the first *berakhah* before the *Shema;* continuing with our recognition of the special relationship of Israel and God, founded on a special kind of love, in the *V'ahavta;* continuing in the next paragraph of the *Shema* to recognize the content of that love as contained in God's teachings, and the need for us to be obedient both to those teachings and to that love; and finally, in the last paragraph of the *Shema* and in the *Emet Ve-yatziv* blessing, concluding with the recognition of the meaning of redemption and, more importantly, the knowledge that we are already redeemed. But this is not a conclusion. It is a beginning. For if we have indeed learned that we are redeemed, then we must go further and learn how to live within such a redeemed vision of the world. That theme will be developed next, in the *Amidah* itself.

As we wrote above, the *Amidah* functions within the liturgy as the replacement for the sacrificial offerings in the Temple. This determines, in large part, its placement in the liturgy as well as the affect the worshiper is expected to bring to its recitation. The *Amidah* is also called *Ha-tefillah,* "*the* prayer" par excellence, in recognition of its extraordinary liturgical importance. Before reciting the *Amidah,* the worshiper steps back and then forward, and this is intended to evoke the priest entering into the chamber of the altar. More metaphorically, it also evokes the worshiper's entering into the presence of God, and the various places in the *Amidah* at which the worshiper bows serve the same purpose. The function of the prayer is then intimately associated with the function of the sacrifice: to achieve atonement, which is the necessary precursor to the onset of redemption.

Mussar discipline attempts to provide opportunities for repentance and atonement, in order that we may reach past those spiritual/intellectual acts to regain or reconnect with love. So too does the *Amidah* allow the worshiper the daily opportunity to effect atonement, for the same reason. As an act of religious imagination, however, the *Amidah* goes even further. Through the opening three *berakhot,* it brings the worshiper to effectively experience what this redemption feels like. In the third *berakhah,* the *Kedushah,* the worshiper actually stands together with groups of angels, whose task it is to eternally sing praises to the Holy One. Each group of angels is given a verse to chant, and so we human beings are also given a verse to chant. Our verse is: "Adonai will reign forever; your God, Zion, from generation to generation" (Psalm 146:10). If we look at the literary context of this psalm, and particularly the verses leading up to this concluding declaration, we will see what the Rabbis believed were the tasks by which human beings truly could fulfill their eternal role in the universe:

> God keeps faith forever,
> Brings justice to the oppressed,
> And provides food for the hungry.
> Adonai frees the bound,
> Adonai gives sight to the blind;
> Adonai raises those bowed down, and loves the just.
> Adonai protects the stranger
> And supports the orphan and widow,
> Adonai frustrates the designs of the wicked.

This is the set of human behaviors that simultaneously effect God's presence in the world and also fulfill the human experience of living in an already redeemed world. Recalling this experience imaginatively motivates us, as we come to terms with the fact that we have not yet achieved such a world. The rest of the *Amidah* is concerned with the human needs that must be addressed in order to bring about such a redeemed world. The thirteen intermediate *berakhot* address the need for knowledge, repentance, forgiveness, mercy, healing, stewardship of nature, freedom, justice, truth, scholarship, true worship, restoration of Israel to its land and holy places, messianic vision, and, finally, the attention of the Other. These values, liturgically formulated as Israel's plea before God, are the necessary values of a world redeemed. The *Amidah* concludes with blessings of thanksgiving and a vision of peace that crowns redemption.

This, then, is the progress of the *Shaḥarit* liturgy: It describes the grand journey of the human soul. This journey begins in response to the love implicit in creation, then moves on toward the responsibility of the human as an agent with God in helping to transform the world, and concludes in a bold vision of redemption. Throughout this journey, obligation is the central content of love and love is the central content of existence. This content comes from beyond the boundaries of mere existence, but it focuses our religious consciousness on the intimate connection between the physical and spiritual well-being of those who pray together in community. This is the Mussar sensibility that animates our approach to prayer. This is why prayer cannot be only voluntary, why it must insist its way into the rhythm of our daily routine. Regular daily prayer is a significant factor in establishing wakefulness in our lives.

This chapter has closely reviewed the required liturgy for its Mussar content and its Mussar discipline. We now turn to other considerations related to prayer: non-liturgical prayer, as well as halakhic ramifications of changing the established order of prayer.

If we recognize that prayer is the essential mechanism for giving voice both to the cry of the suffering and to the command to attend to that cry, then prayer must always remain fluid, even amidst its traditional fixed form. The voice of the stranger, the one who has had no voice in the established community, may be able to interrupt the accepted cadence of community prayer, and we must remain open to this possibility. Another possibility is that even those who have been regular participants in the life of the community's prayer may discover within themselves a new need— either a need that has never before been articulated, or a need previously articulated that has never before been attended to. For these reasons, spontaneous prayer has always been a very legitimate complement to the traditional, fixed prayer structure. Such spontaneous prayer can take the form of private additions to and around the public prayer service. It can also emerge at any time or place that the need occurs.

A more serious issue in the life of the community are the ways in which the prayer service can be changed. Certainly throughout history Jewish communities have articulated their particular needs and the needs of their members by adding *piyyutim* (poems) or *kavanot* (meditations) to the prayer service. Such additions, when sanctioned by community consensus, are to be lauded. Often, in the contemporary prayer service, the primary value for many worshipers is the brevity of the service. This may be because these worshipers do not know the meaning of the words they are reciting. Alternatively, even if these worshipers do understand the words, they may not take the time necessary to allow the words to emerge from the depths of their souls, or to accost their souls in such a way that they open themselves to the voice crying out to them. The technique of Mussar study with lips aflame, described above (in chapter 10), was derived at least in part from the method of prayer-internalization that had been so prevalent among previous generations of Jews. In the contemporary synagogue, we are left either with a parody of this technique of *davening* or with a recitative style that is drained of all emotion. For generations of Jews who preceded us, the time spent in prayer was not measured in minutes but in tears. It is perhaps the case not that we pray for too long, but that we pray for not long enough. Were we to be sensitized to the cry and the command emerging from true prayer, we might again feel called to remain in its sphere rather than to flee it. There might then emerge any number of additions to our present service. Certainly the number of voices and the number of burdens assaulting the human community is not diminishing!

It is clearly within the parameters of the tradition to add to the public prayer service when the need to do so arises, and also to remove these additions when they are no longer relevant. Beyond this, however, the question of changes within the body of the accepted, authoritative prayer texts requires further examination. Mussar consciousness would certainly require the community's authentic voice to include in it the pain of each of its members and the command to respond to the suffering of any of its members. Therefore, as a community becomes more sensitive to the pain of those whose voices are not reflected in the traditional text, it must be prepared to rectify this omission. In many contemporary Jewish communities, this has already occurred regarding the voices of women. Yet other voices still remain excluded from our midst and from our prayers. We should feel encouraged to participate in this process, working against the background of an always imperfect present and against a forever receding perfect future, as we slowly learn to bear more and more of the burden of the other.

CHAPTER SEVENTEEN

Becoming a Revelation

The wakefulness that characterizes Mussar leads to a condition of on-going transformation. We have seen how the *emotional* aspect of human consciousness may be transformed through prayer. This occurs as the expression of infinite longing for an Infinite Beloved, and as the response to the cry of another's suffering translated into bearing the burden of those who suffer. *Talmud torah* is the corresponding transformation of our *intellectual* aspect by wakefulness.

All creatures act in ways that increase their ultimate pleasure through refinement of the intellect. The actions and thoughts of all creatures are grounded in instinctive behavior, but education—even at its simplest level—can allow creatures to use their instincts to maximize pleasure. Beginning with survival itself but reaching far beyond mere survival, creatures of the world learn skills that facilitate pleasure. For humans, the action of another responding to our earliest needs brings us into consciousness of our existence. The other, and our knowledge of another, are the basic building blocks of our intellect. However, the role of the other tends to become overshadowed during the development of our intellect, insofar as this knowledge functions primarily in enabling us to pursue our own pleasure. In fact, a forgetfulness regarding the other's presence in the core of our intellectual experience is, at some stages of our development, necessary. Sleep is an inevitable and necessary element of existence in this world. However, Mussar requires the quest for wakefulness, and the wakefulness of the intellect is achieved through *talmud torah.*

The phrase *talmud torah* is derived from the Oral Torah. It is a complex expression that includes the ideas of "teaching revelation" and "learning revelation," but at its heart it means "living revelation." Through *talmud torah,* we take in information and transform those thoughts into action, striving to better enjoy our existence. A primary form of human enjoyment is seeking the good of another, and this is certainly a goal for human beings according to both the Oral and Written Torah. However, in order to fully appreciate the centrality of *talmud torah* in Jewish tradition (and especially its centrality in Mussar consciousness), we must look more closely at what the term means. The complexity of the word *talmud*—this admixture of the English words "learn," "teach," and even "contemplate"—pales in comparison to the complexity of the word *torah.* We have already touched on the meaning of this latter term, but we should not be surprised at the necessity of examining it again. It is the central word of Jewish experience.

Torah is so central to Mussar consciousness because of how Torah solicits our desire to acquire more Torah. Torah is, first and foremost, that which we acquire in the construction of our consciousness by bearing the burden of our neighbor. We become who we are, we forge our souls, by responding to this infinite call that stands outside of ourselves but, at the same time, constitutes the innermost core of our being. Torah is the call that makes us human, and that defines what we mean when we speak about revelation. Wakefulness is what allows us to transform the call itself into our obsessive concern with responding to it. *Talmud torah* is the obsessive concern with hearing the call, and that concern is what makes us human. The call commands us to bear the burden of our neighbor and it elects us to shoulder our responsibilities for another, through the minute details of living everyday in the world. We speak of *talmud torah* as an activity that must persist day and night and we pray: ". . . the words which I have placed in your mouth shall not be absent from your mouth, nor from the mouth of your children, nor from the mouth of your children's children" (Isaiah 59:21, as incorporated into the daily prayer service). This language reflects the wakefulness of discovering the ever more commanding call, of accepting our responsibility to bear the burden of another. Our obsession with Torah is an obsession with our responsibility. It is an obsession with the call that makes us human. It is an obsession with living in the constant echo of revelation.

We have discussed earlier the fact that "Torah" is a complex idea. Torah has a content that descended upon the Jewish people as soon as Abraham and Sarah began to hear the call of the burden of the other, and it exploded into the consciousness of an entire nation at Sinai. Torah also has a history, and the constant search to better hear and better implement the words of the Torah through *halakhah* forms an important part of Jewish spirituality. But the *talmud torah* that we address here in the flow of Mussar spirituality is not about *halakhah*. It derives from the notion of *torah lishmah,* Torah-learning for its own sake. *Talmud torah* is the act of studying Torah, the obsession with studying the texts of the written and oral tradition. Moreover, it is a central tenet of Mussar that *talmud torah* must ultimately transcend the informational content of those texts, allowing us to transform ideas into action.

The human intellect is comprised of the presence of the other, our knowledge of the presence of the other, and the capacity to use reason to move beyond mere survival to enjoyment of life. The healthy development of the individual requires that we sometimes forget about the presence of the other, so that we may develop sufficient passion for ourselves. However, as the intellect develops, it must come to realize that an individual's ultimate enjoyment is embodied in bearing the burden of another, a beloved who eventually becomes an Infinite Beloved. An intellect that develops this way will hear the call of Torah and will derive more and more of its pleasure by assuming more and more responsibility for another. It will want to fill itself with the ceaseless source of this call. The Mussar-oriented individual will, encouraged by the force of wakefulness, turn to the texts of the Torah with a passionate desire to live within both the demands and the history of this call. To study Torah every day, every minute of the day; to speak words of Torah at every moment—these are the goals of Mussar spirituality, because in their fulfillment lies the fulfillment of the human intellect itself.

Studying Torah day and night means positioning oneself at every moment to acquire Torah, which is itself a function of bearing the burden of another. To live a life of *talmud torah* is to live revelation, by allowing revelation to position us vis-à-vis our neighbor in such a way that we are prepared to bear their burden. This is why *talmud torah* is central to Mussar consciousness.

Clearly, the disjunction between Mussar intellectual consciousness and the intellectual consciousness of contemporary Jews is severe. In contemporary culture we are taught to empty our intellect of the presence of the other and to use our reason almost exclusively to work toward our own pleasure. This emphasis has produced a world capable of providing more pleasure to more people in more ways than could ever have been imagined. We benefit from many miracles brought into existence by the power of human reason—such as advances in modern medicine, in communication and transportation, and in technology (all of which lighten the burdens of human labor). Many of these accomplishments

derive from a latent concern for the other, which is embedded in
the core of our early intellectual development; indeed, many of
these miracles provide for the care of so many individuals. We cannot and should not dismiss these accomplishments. But when we
eventually come to realize that the world created by this reason has
gone askew, we are plagued by an insistent feeling that something
is missing. The insistence of this lack is the experience of evil. In
response to this insistence, we reconstitute our intellectual framework to again include within it ample room to acquire Torah,
which is the bearing of the burden of the other. The contemporary
Jew whose intellect is stuck on the level of seeking pleasure, not
recognizing that its true pleasure is derived from bearing the burden of the other, needs a remedy. This remedy is *talmud torah* and
especially *torah lishmah,* learning Torah for the sake of the spiritual
sustenance it provides. The contemporary Jew whose intellect
refuses to work toward increasing the physical well-being of the
other, who rejects reason and hides behind the texts of Torah to
avoid taking responsibility for another, is also stuck. However, the
contemporary Jew whose intellect is committed to the accomplishments of reason within the context of acquiring Torah can
truly be called a *talmid ḥakham,* a sage.

Studying traditional texts via the wakefulness of *torah lishmah*
sufficed for generations of Jews as their entryway into the life of
revelation. But ours is not the first generation of Jews for whom
these texts often appear at first to be impediments, rather than aids,
to spirituality. Until we can appreciate that the often arcane and
intricate discussions of law—often law that has no immediate
application to our lives—masks an obsessive concern with developing an awareness of our responsibility for others, these texts can
appear closed to us. For this reason, Mussar practice makes more
room for texts that are explicitly concerned with the obsessive
concern for another and our responsibilities to bear the burden of

another alongside traditional rabbinic texts. Where the classical texts of Rabbinic Judaism reflect a reading of the Written Torah through the optic of Mussar, these texts are used. Rabbinic texts may encourage us to refine the very power of our reason, but Mussar texts are more concerned with getting to the heart of our task. The study of the more recondite texts may become so difficult that the goal of our study becomes obfuscated, but Mussar texts will keep the goal always before our eyes. Thus the traditional Torah curriculum, in the Mussar context, was modified to include these texts alongside the traditional rabbinic texts.

The founders of the Mussar movement understood the power of secular learning, recognizing that it represented both a good in itself (insofar as it resulted in intellectual discoveries, which brought great good to great numbers of people) and also a worthy challenger for the attention of students. They therefore included such studies in their curriculum. Adding both secular studies and Mussar texts to the traditional curriculum was a radical act that drew strong criticism from the traditional Jewish community. However, the wisdom of their willingness to introduce change, as well as the mandate for such an approach in our own time, ought to embolden us to likewise add to our notion of *talmud torah* and *torah lishmah*; both secular study of the highest caliber and the study of Mussar texts should be included in any modern approach to Jewish learning. The latter serves an independent good and also serves as a protective framework in which the former unfolds. The development of a contemporary Mussar spirituality requires the development of a contemporary *talmud torah* and *torah lishmah*.

CHAPTER EIGHTEEN

Making Space for Eternity

In the opening paragraph of Rav Simḥa Zissel's *Ḥokhmah U-Mussar* we encountered an idea which is of central importance to the theology of Mussar consciousness: ". . . All of them [the forty-eight steps by which Torah is acquired, according to Avot 6:1] taken together instill in one a new nature, that of being 'master of a fine soul'—one fit for Torah and wisdom to be attached to, as a result of which one's soul is bound up with the bond of eternal life." In other words, eternal life is not linearly related to life in this world as we know it. Thus, for example, the term "afterlife" is misleading since the "world to come" is not a temporal concept. Rather, this world and the world of eternity co-exist and are co-terminus—one might almost say parallel. The possibility exists at any and every moment for this world to be punctuated by the promise of the world to come. The agent of this potential is the act of acquiring Torah which, as we've seen, is a consequence of bearing the burden of another. The possibility that this world can be entirely transformed at any moment exists and the responsibility for whether it will or will not be so transformed lies in our hands. This is the power of this theology: It is a powerful religious humanism by which the very possibility for eternity depends entirely on our actions. For the contemporary Jew, the particulars of the language that expresses this humanism may seem quaint. However, the challenge that the language carries is anything but quaint. It challenges the sense of powerlessness in the face of evil that characterizes the present age. To recognize that human beings do indeed have power—that transforming the world *is* in our hands and that accepting the responsibility of being human is the first and most important step in accessing this power—challenges our very notion of what it means to be alive. In the wake of the tragedies of the past centuries, it may seem at best a naïve view of humanity and at worst a dangerous illusion.

Yet, the radical assertion of Jewish experience, perhaps the most radical, is that aspects of eternity can indeed be experienced within the structure of this-worldly time. Time itself can be interrupted by eternity and timelessness can carve a space for itself in the midst of time. Beyond simply making this assertion, Jewish life provides regular opportunities for experiencing such eternal interruptions in time. The mysterious narrative of Jewish experience, the Torah that calls us from outside of ourselves, is interwoven with eternity-like interruptions from its very beginning. As the world is brought into existence by the love of an Other for it, and as this world is called "good" and "very good," the narrative of this beginning is interrupted by the establishment of the Sabbath, which will serve as a trace of the eternal within the very structure of time. The Sabbath will provide an opportunity for people to experience the reality of eternity in the midst of their temporal lives, wherever they are and whatever they are doing. The centrality of the Sabbath to Jewish experience cannot be overstated. From the creation story to the description of the Sinai event, from the details of observance spelled out in the wilderness narrative to the details of worship described in the priestly codes, the Sabbath is the central theological pillar of Jewish life. Without this experience of the possibility of transforming the world by interrupting the flow of time, even the mandate to acquire Torah and to bear the burden of the other would lose their moorings.

The Sabbath is so central to Jewish experience that this interruption of the eternal into the temporal became the defining characteristic of Jews' experience of their own history and of nature. Thus, the liberation of Israel from slavery in Egypt, the encounter between God and Israel at Sinai, and wandering in the wilderness while entirely dependent on Another, are all expressed through the observance of Sabbath-like occasions—namely, the Festivals. And these historical events are, in turn, superimposed onto the experiences of gratitude occasioned by the three major harvest periods in the ancient Israelite calendar. Jews experience both history and nature as manifestations of the obsessive concern of the Other for humanity, as interruptions of eternity into time that *can* be experienced by human beings. God's love for Israel, as expressed in history and through nature, precipitates the Sabbath and Festivals. And the Sabbath and Festivals then become both memorial to that love and inspiration for the human power to transform the world, such that the interruption of time into eternity and back again will eventually cease, and we will transform the world into a state of perpetual eternity.

CHAPTER NINETEEN

Hyperbole and Messianism

At this point, we briefly revisit the practical ramifications of the Mussar theology that we have described on the basis of the teachings of Rav Simḥa Zissel of Kelm, in order to build the bridge between theory and practice. The primary theoretical technique of Rav Simḥa is the establishment of a hyperbolic ethic, which then precipitates the creation of the all-important imaginative projection. By stretching ethics beyond the bounds of ordinary behavior, by forging an ethic so powerful and all-consuming that it defines the very existence of the individuality of the human being, Rav Simḥa attempts to create an unbearable pressure on the individual to view the world through the optic of this hyperbolic ethic. He makes this move despite the fact that functioning on the hyperbolic plane is practically impossible. The very attempt to glimpse the world through the lens of this hyperbole is, precisely because of its impossibility, an experience that bursts the confines of rationalism without rejecting reason as such. The hyperbolic is not reasonable. It does not conform to the canons of conventionality. It serves as another intrusion of wakefulness into an otherwise slumbering world, a slumbering soul. Ethics, in this context, is no longer merely the practical task of choosing right behavior. Right behavior will always depend on the specific circumstances in which one finds oneself. Right behavior is a matter of *halakhah* and, as such, is constantly open to interpretation. This realization that ethical behavior cannot always be known in advance and cannot be determined by fiat is itself part of the process of living within the ethical hyperbole. Internalizing the hyperbolic stance effects the desired transformation of individuals into people who are committed to striving for right behavior, always aware that in doing so they are taking risks and must therefore maintain a judicious humility. The particular hyperbole of this ethic is the unceasing responsibility to bear the burden of another. To achieve the carrying of this burden fully, not only for *one* other but for *every* other, cannot be accomplished in the world structured as we know it. But the presence of the mandate to achieve that goal allows for the possibility of a world structured in a way we do not yet know, and also provides a measure of just how close we might come to effecting this transformation from the world we know to the world we do not.

Within the context of traditional Jewish theology, this hyperbolic ethic serves precisely the same purpose as that of messianism. The unique insight of Mussar theology, however, concerns the transformation of the idea of the messianic expectation into an explicitly ethical tool. This is not to say that the messianic idea in Judaism has not already, from its inception, entailed a strong ethical content. On the contrary, the messianic idea is predicated on the possibility of the victory of good over evil, even when such a victory appears to be impossible. However, the perspective of Mussar consciousness not only makes the implicit ethical content of messianism explicit, but it also links this content to the very humanity of a human being. The concept of messianism thus moves beyond a simple understanding of the end toward which humanity is moving, to encompass also the power out of which humanity emerged.

In the end, both expressions of this same phenomenon—hyperbolic ethics and messianism—are grounded in the core idea of redemption in Jewish life. From the Exodus from Egypt to the expected end-of-days, the idea of redemption lies at the heart of the Jewish worldview. The sine qua non of Jewish theology is that as Jews, we live in a world that has experienced redemption. The centrality of the Exodus story (especially its liturgical prominence) posits that we have already undergone a truly transformative experience. We have already experienced the "outstretched arm" that has answered our cry. The meaning of that experience is never in doubt: to care for the widow and orphan and the stranger because "you were strangers in a strange land." The messianic hope is that the redemption of the past will be re-enacted in the future. The hyperbolic ethic of Mussar lives in the responsibility incumbent upon an already redeemed people who have it in their hands to make moments of that redemption endlessly manifest.

Appendix

Ḥokhmah U-Mussar
Translation and Commentary

okhmah U-Mussar is divided into chapters comprised
mostly of transcriptions of Mussar talks and letters from
Rav Simḥa Zissel to his students. Each chapter is further divided into paragraphs, which I have numbered in my translation. Some of the selections are followed by addenda, which I
have labeled either Addendum or Coda. I will begin here with
some general comments regarding Rav Simḥa Zissel's work, and
will then proceed with a paragraph-by-paragraph annotation of
the first five chapters of the work.

It is important to begin by noting that Rav Simḥa works foremost as a commentator. That is, he purports to find insights, offered
from within a specific body of texts that are already recognized by
his audience as authoritative. By accepting these texts as authoritative, he is free to read them anew. He thus places himself in a tradition of re-reading that is always trying to recover an original
meaning—a past which is his, but which he could not have experienced. The historical period in which Rav Simḥa worked certainly allowed for different choices of how to approach texts. In
fact, Rav Simḥa's work may have been motivated (at least in part)

precisely by the spread of the *Haskalah* in Russia at the time: Since many other reading strategies were now seen as legitimate, Rav Simḥa needed to develop a methodology from within the tradition. Rav Simḥa's work, nevertheless, contains an implicit critique and admission that the tradition's "truth" required such a re-reading, that the tradition required the development of a hermeneutics, of an ethics.

The tradition out of which Rav Simḥa worked is enormous. His reading juggles biblical, classical rabbinic, and medieval texts together with kabbalistic learning. His method consists of weaving a narrative, seamlessly connecting elements of this tradition in such a way as to demonstrate in the narrative structure itself just those values that the content of the narrative recommends. That is to say, the act of studying Mussar will and must be an ethical act, an act whereby one bears the burden of the other. As we will see, the act of bearing the burden of the other is first, and perhaps primarily, an act that requires a new way of seeing the world—what we will call an imaginative projection into the world from the perspective of the other or of God. Since one must actually accomplish such a projection in studying *Ḥokhmah U-Mussar,* this study itself is the first Mussar act. The first ethical act is interpretation.

The specific principles of interpretation that have the power to ground such an ethics are imaginative projection and also excessive concern for the other, which we will call "hyperbolic ethics." The development and usefulness of these principles are best observed within the narrative. However, for introductory purposes, we shall clarify their meaning. The act we have called "imaginative projection" does indeed involve a new way of seeing the world, either through the eyes of the other or of God. However, to leave it at that would leave us feeling slightly betrayed by the promise of Rav Simḥa's work. Is not the suggestion that we

can see the world through the eyes of the other really just another
way of saying that we can make the other's eyes our own—that
the other can be made into the same? This would certainly be the
case, if not for the specific vision that Rav Simḥa contends is
available to us by applying this principle of imaginative projection: namely, a vision that is always and only the bearing of the
burden of the other. This is a vision that weighs on us, a vision in
which we can only take upon ourselves the pain of the other.
Nothing else of the other is visible to our eyes; everything but the
pain is opaque. To believe that we can see anything else through
the other's eyes is to see nothing. Moreover, this is what is meant
when we say that God "sees" human beings. God "sees" human
beings by vouchsafing to humans the ability to bear the burden of
their fellow. We will observe Rav Simḥa's method at arriving at
this startling principle below.

The principle we have called "hyperbolic ethics" flows from
this first principle. Rav Simḥa reads the texts of the tradition "as
if" this concern blotted out every and any other possible concern
we could have. It is a concern so intolerably heavy that it demands
God's assistance in carrying it. The very weight of our burden and
our attempts to shoulder it introduce us, as it were, to God. Only
the bearing the burden of the other, in fact, accomplishes this step
on the way to God. However, the only aspect of God that we can
experience is God's own giving to us the perspective of bearing
the burden. Does Rav Simḥa mean to suggest that no talk of
God—other than about this aspect of God—makes any sense?
Does he maintain that no other aspect of God (without denying
that there must be other aspects of God) can be comprehended by
human beings? The hyperbolic nature of his language would certainly suggest this. Yet, by its precise nature as hyperbole, it refuses
to entirely preclude competing possibilities. What he most certain-

ly is suggesting is simply a matter of priority. No other speculation about God can take priority over the God who is apprehended in our bearing the burden of the other, without denying the sure encounter with God in the revelation of Torah. Teaching this doctrine, by extension, is itself transformed into an ethical act.

Chapter One: "Sweet and Beautiful"

I Our Sages taught: One of the methods by which the Torah is acquired is by carrying the burden of our fellow. Each of the [48] steps that they enumerate there (Avot 6) are like preliminary goals, achieved by following each step, in order to bring about the ultimate goal. All of them taken together instill in one a new nature—that of being "master of a fine soul"—one fit for Torah and wisdom to be attached to, as a result of which one's soul is bound up with the bond of eternal life. Without this it is impossible to acquire Torah, for it is a spiritual entity and cannot attach itself to one who does not merit it on account of one's continuing pre-occupation with material matters.

Rav Simḥa begins his essay by focusing on one of forty-eight personality qualities (*middot*) that Pirke Avot sees as necessary for one to "acquire" Torah (i.e., binding the spiritual force of Torah to the human soul). It is a common Jewish mystical notion that the physical Torah is but a "cover" for a spiritual (or supernal) Torah: the literal Torah "hides" a more purely spiritual vehicle. Rav Simḥa's reading of Avot is no more literal than his understanding of the Torah. Although Avot seems to consider these *middot* as all equally important, Rav Simḥa claims that "carrying the burden with one's fellow" is the goal of all the rest; reaching this goal testifies to the transformation of one's human nature into a spiritual nature transcending death itself. It is to this transformed infinite soul, whose infinity is effected by bearing the pain of others, that the spiritual Torah adheres.

We might, therefore, suggest that the relationship between the finite and the infinite, between the enclosed self and the other, is bridged by assuming responsibility one for the other. The introduction of infinity (or eternity) into this equation, though not unexpected in a religious document, itself suggests an obligation that precedes the self, an obligation toward the other. In a very real sense then, the Torah is only brought into the world by the bearing of the burden of the other. Simultaneously, the soul itself comes into being by attaching itself to this Torah, which itself came into existence by virtue of bearing of the burden of the other. Creation of the individual as a material existent (a given in this world) is thus transformed by Torah—what we can already call revelation, a command to guide us toward redemption. This must be redemption not of ourselves but of the other, whose burden we bear.

II   To reach the level of being one who bears the burden of one's fellow is impossible unless one has accustomed oneself to love one's neighbor in thought and deed. However, whereas the deeds of most people are observable, their thoughts are not. In order to ascertain that one loves one's neighbor in both deed and thought two criteria must be used. First we must examine the consequences of deeds and thoughts both, to be sure that they are politically constructive, for it is the political structure that sustains the world and, conversely, can shatter it. This is the lesson we learn from the destruction of the Temple, which was destroyed on account of unbridled social enmity. Since the Temple was the knot holding the world together, maintained by the treasured people, when they sinned it was

**erased and immediately the Temple shattered in this world.
May the Exalted One return it to us speedily!**

Rav Simḥa claims that the love of one's fellow human being
is, in fact, the defining quality equal to bearing the burden of
one's fellow. Moreover, he teaches that we cannot judge love of
one's neighbors by acts alone, though judging acts is obviously
easier than judging thoughts. To ascertain the quality of love one
has for others, we must judge thoughts also. Finally, he teaches in
no uncertain terms that the criteria by which both thoughts and
acts of love are judged is social, in the sense that an act has ramifications beyond the self: Living in this world is thus fused with a
sense of responsibility to others. Rav Simḥa learns this from the
traditional explanation for the destruction of the Temple—namely, enmity in the social weal—and he draws out from this social
idea certain implications for spiritual life. The Temple was the
knot that united the material and the spiritual. Social injustice
caused the erasure or untying of this knot.

In this remarkable foray into the world of history and politics,
Rav Simḥa confronts the question of the meaning and the telos of
history. History is suffering, he says. The lot of man-in-exile is
social alienation. In these ideas we can surely recognize important
questions of late nineteenth- and early twentieth-century Jews. Just
as clearly, Rav Simḥa upholds the notion that love of one's fellow
must express itself in thought and in deed, deeds which materially
affect one's lot. Why the emphasis on thought? Because the potential of deeds toward the other to be either oppressive or redemptive depends entirely on the analysis that generates the deeds—the
imaginative projection from which they flow. We might have
expected a radical ethics to be concerned primarily with deeds,
but Rav Simḥa insists that in and of themselves deeds can be misleading. The analysis or thought, the imaginative projection that

inevitably must produce deeds, is the first ethics—an ethics that is also a politics. The state (or community) flows from the proper imaginative projection of the individuals within that state (or community). Moses, who will later be introduced as the paradigmatic possessor of the proper imaginative projection, is also Moses the lawgiver, the founder of the social structure.

> **III   It is impossible to love the other as oneself until one has removed all traces of materiality. Those who find no mixture of materiality in themselves can then unify the parts of their soul. In reality there are no divisions in the spirit that are not caused by materiality, as the verse implies: "To satisfy one's own vanity" (Proverbs 18:1) means "one divides oneself."**

The division between the material and the spiritual is determined not by correspondence to nature, but by the actions of the self in the world. Rav Simha teaches that to love another, which has already been described as a step on the way toward assuming the burden of the other, cannot be accomplished unless one rids oneself of all traces of materiality. But this "materiality" is the dross of consciousness, not the physical body of a person. Vanity is the cause of the division of the self into the "material" and the "spiritual." It is certainly not the physical nature of creation that our emerging Mussar spirituality critiques, since our spirituality expresses itself through concern for the other's physical needs. Rather, the pernicious division of the human being, the interior battle, is between vanity and responsibility. Materialism is a function of attitude, not of resources.

Rav Simha's use of the trope of materiality seems to mean the need to fulfill material wants, as a necessary prerequisite to suffering the surplus of desire that maintains itself after these needs are fulfilled. Thus, we have an entirely new—but, I think, remarkably accurate—framework in which to read this common kabbalistic notion. Within this framework, the notion of the divided self can be re-read as the self seeking satisfaction. As long as the self is seeking its own satisfaction (which is a necessary and unavoidable process), that self is divided, or perhaps even weighted down by its materiality. Removing all traces of such materiality cannot mean not living in the material world, for Rav Simha is certainly talking about real flesh and blood people. Rather, it must mean people for whom the search for self-satisfaction, material satisfaction, is no longer primary. These people have unified their souls, surpassed their neediness, and it is as though they were without materiality. In concluding this thought, we notice that this search for the unified self is grounded in the search for the person who loves the other, and this love of the other is an expression of the social world.

IV We have already introduced the idea that a person's cleaving to the spiritual Torah is impossible unless that person has become a person of spirit—that is, one in whom there is a true unified soul. Our Sages well understood that "To love your neighbor as yourself, this is the great principle of the Torah" (Genesis Rabbah 24:8). For a person of spirit, the master of a fine soul, the soul is attached to the Torah through love, through observance in thought and deed. Such a love enables the crude materiality of one's nature to undergo a thorough spiritual cleansing.

Rav Simha here explains that the biblical verse "Love your neighbor as yourself" is precisely about "bearing the burden of the other"—and that this is indeed *the* "great principle" of the Torah. For Rav Simha, there would be no Torah were it not for this love, which is the bearing of the burden of the other. The Torah would, as it were, remain unattached to the human soul. It might exist, but its existence would be hidden, meaningless from the human perspective. At the same time, without this love (which is the bearing of the burden of the other), there would also be no true human being. What we can rightfully call "human being" is precisely that mode of existence effected by bearing another's burden. This love purifies the soul. It makes the human "master of a fine soul"—that is, one who has attained mastery over the self's physical needs and is therefore able to give oneself up to become attached to Torah, to and through love of another. Yet, this love comes to us as a command, an imperative: "Love your neighbor as yourself!" It comes from outside the self and, revealing itself as our obligation, it creates us as human beings. We, who are masters of the fine soul, submit to the command. This Rav Simḥa calls spiritual cleansing.

V   There is another aspect regarding the specific education of one who bears the burden of the other, about which our Sages taught in beautiful and fanciful language. Our Sages said in Bava Metzia (page 83b): "'You make darkness and it is night (Psalm 104:20)'—this refers to this world, which is similar to night." By this they meant that the interior of the world is hidden in this world. "'Wherein all the beasts of the forest creep forth'—these are the evil ones, since they are as though perpetually in the forest." What wisdom and understanding come to us by this metaphor describing evil ones as "perpetually in the forest"? We learn from this an essential insight regarding the education of a person: namely, that it is impossible to come to feel the suffering of the other, to carry another's burden, except by creating an internal perception so that the trouble, the pain, the suffering of the other (God forbid!) were one's own pain. Therefore, all that we would expect one to do to bear one's own pain, we ask for one to do for the other. Only in this way does one come to the level of bearing

the burden of the other. It is known that a wild animal will only attack those that are domesticated. Thus are the evil ones like wild beasts—meaning that they are far from having any interior perception of the other, and therefore they are unable to feel the pain of the other. We learn all these insights indirectly (not as the main focus of the talmudic argument, but by inference from the way the verses are treated) from the holy and embellished language of the Sages.

In this paragraph Rav Simḥa turns to the pedagogical element of his system for the first time. He will develop, throughout these chapters, a pedagogic imperative: teaching becomes an ethical act. Studying Mussar, however, must precede teaching. Studying is an initial experience of love (i.e., bearing the burden of the other). However, the first outward movement of this love, the first response to the command to love, is to teach.

Rav Simḥa reaches this pedagogic imperative by continuing to interpret. He focuses on a statement in the Talmud that is itself already interpreting a verse in the Bible. Rav Simḥa calls this talmudic interpretation "a beautiful and fanciful" teaching, a phrase that recalls (and perhaps explains) the title of this first essay, "Sweet and Beautiful." It certainly suggests that the talmudic passage in question is to be read not literally but as containing hidden wisdom. The title may also suggest that we cannot read Rav Simḥa's work any more literally than he reads the Talmud—or, for that matter, than the Talmud reads Scripture.

The talmudic passage that Rav Simḥa interprets here is in a section of the Talmud that addresses the Mishnah's law about treating hired laborers. Much of the Mishnah deals with the requirement to provide appropriate food for the laborers, which depends in part on local custom. In the course of the talmudic discussion,

Psalm 104 is quoted: "You make darkness, and it is night; wherein all the beasts of the forest creep forth." The Sages in the Talmud say that "You make darkness, and it is night" refers to *this* world, which is comparable to night. Rav Simḥa uncovers in this interpretation not that this world literally unfolds in darkness, but rather that there is a hidden world that resides within this world. He continues with the talmudic exposition, according to which the phrase "wherein all the beasts of the forest creep forth" describes those who are evil, for they are in a perpetual forest. Who are these evil ones? According to Rav Simḥa, they are those who are unable to come to feel the suffering of the other. They are unable to feel this pain because they are unable to create the appropriate imaginative projection. The otherwise hidden imaginative projection, which we cannot actually see but must imagine and then see, in fact defines that which is hidden beneath the structure of the world. The task of education, then, is to bring the evil ones out of the darkness of the forest by allowing them to perceive the hidden world of God's creation, which is the bearing of the burden of the other. The darkness of the world, the forest in which the evil ones find themselves trapped, is the inability to imagine the pain of the other and to bear it as if it were one's own.

Finally, Rav Simḥa extends the talmudic metaphor of "wild beasts" by noting that such beasts are most dangerous because they attack those that are domesticated. He seems to mean that the image of the evil ones hidden or in the forest describes not only their existential state but also the danger they pose to those who are innocent. Education must, therefore, assume that each student needs to be taken out of the "forest," out of the darkness and into the light. This is itself an ethical act, an act of love toward the evil one as other. We bear their burden just as we teach them to bear the burden of others.

VI One should increase one's perceptions in matters that cannot be certain, like those of the past and, all the more so, of the future. For they come to enlighten us, since it is the way of wisdom to investigate thoroughly these matters in order to understand their end. For this reason the Sages said: "Who is wise? The one who sees the consequences of a situation" (Tamid 32a). This means that one always holds a perception of the future against oneself.

The imaginative projection that results in the bearing of the burden of the other comes carrying the past and marking the horizon of the future. In this rather cryptic paragraph Rav Simḥa expands the utility of imaginative projection, by what we could almost call a type of meditative thinking. This allows one to open up one's own past, which approaches on the shoulders of the other whose burden one bears. More importantly, this meditation also opens a way to the future. This future, in classic Levinasian language, is a future that comes to me by virtue of its being another's future, and therefore is always a surprise for me. The horizon of this future must be the death of the other and my implication in this death, insofar as I do not bear the burden of their pain (and, in fact, even if I do).

Rav Simḥa uses this opportunity to define wisdom. We must keep in mind that *ḥokhmah,* wisdom (or contemplation), must be considered a significant theme of his work, even appearing as half the title of his book. His reference to the passage in Tamid for a definition of wisdom is especially interesting, since a variant of this saying appears in the much better known tractate Avot. In Avot we find:

> Ben Zoma said: "Who is wise? The one who learns from every person, as it is stated: 'From all those who have taught me I have gained wisdom; indeed, Your testimonies are my conversation (Psalm 119:99).'"

However, in tractate Tamid this same question introduces a series of questions asked of the Rabbis by Alexander the Great. The answers are similar, but not the same.

> He (Alexander) said to them: "Who is called wise?" They replied: "Who is wise? The one who discerns the consequences of a situation."

We might, at first, be surprised that Rav Simḥa did not choose the better known formulation from Avot, which also seems to naturally follow from his previous paragraph where teaching was established as an ethical imperative. If learning is ethics, shouldn't we learn from everyone? The point is: No. In fact, we are obliquely warned to avoid such a conclusion; we are reminded to carefully foresee the consequences of our actions, including the act of teaching. Achieving the ability to properly construct the necessary imaginative projection requires intense effort. It cannot be the product of happenstance but rather requires deep inquiry. It requires a particular type of teaching, which had been neglected in Rav Simḥa's day. It requires taking students "out of the forest" in which they are trapped. Thus, a wise person is *not* someone who learns from everyone, but instead someone who foresees the consequences of teaching and learning, which are the bearing the burden of the other.

Not accidentally, this particular passage also reminds readers that those who gave this answer were being interrogated, not without a hint of violence, by Alexander the Great. Alexander certainly is a figure symbolic of Hellenism and Greek thought, of enlightenment in all its forms. The reference to Alexander may be a way of telegraphing an aversion to the exclusive claims of contemporary *Haskalah* learning by contemporary Alexanders, the followers of *Haskalah*.

Finally, this statement in Tamid serves as an introduction to the rest of this chapter: Rav Simḥa needs to explain the appropriate type of teaching necessary to Mussar, since one cannot simply learn it from anyone.

> VII   For this reason we have spoken about one comment that has been made concerning a section of the Torah dealing with the manna. We say: How stupid human beings are, for Heaven directs all and yet they worry when they receive their payment about today but they do not worry about tomorrow. The comment, by Ramban in *Parashat Ha-man:*

>> Know that the matter of the manna is very important and is hinted at by our Rabbis of blessed memory also. In tractate Yoma we find: "Man did eat the bread of the mighty" (Psalm 78:25). According to Rabbi Akiva this means that men ate the bread of ministering angels. But Rabbi Yishmael said to him: "You are mistaken, for do the angels eat bread? Rather, bread was absorbed into their limbs." But what Rabbi Akiva meant was that the angels exist by absorbing the light of the Shekhinah, etc. . . . The manna emerges from the same upper lights raining down light upon the angels, and raining down manna upon the Israelites at the will of the blessed Creator. It turns out that the people of the wilderness were sustained by the same substance as the angels, but in a different form. But Rabbi Yishmael holds that the angels are not sustained by this shower of light, but rather by the very light of the Heavens.

> In either case their nourishment is in a spiritual form and emanates from the effulgence of the Shekhinah.

>> The Mekhilta adds that this manna is the food of the world to come—in its form as the effulgence of the

lights from on high, about which our Rabbis taught: "The righteous sit with crowns on their heads and enjoy the effulgence of the Shekhinah" (Berakhot 17a).

This is so regardless of whether we follow Rabbi Akiva or Rabbi Yishmael. Thus, regarding wise people who understand the future and are capable of imaginative projection, how could it be possible that they would not gird themselves to have the strength to wage this war? Would they not prepare the meat and victuals of eternity, that is, enjoying the effulgence of light available through contemplation and Torah, and specifically acquiring Torah in the way most suited for its acquisition (as we have explained), so that in this way they will receive sustenance from the effulgence of the Shekhinah? And if, God forbid, they experience a sadness of soul and become discouraged at the effort required to receive this effulgence, let them consider how much greater will be their suffering and pain for myriads of years without end, should they not prepare themselves to enjoy this effulgence despite the effort.

Paragraph VII is predicated on our understanding that learning Mussar is not like learning anything else, and it is certainly not like learning from everyone or anyone. One reason for this is that most people cannot discern the future. They are the foolish ones who do not know that wisdom is the bearing of the burden of the other, who do not know that this is the meaning of "Love your neighbor as yourself." Teaching is also an act of bearing the burden of the other. All who would teach without bearing the burden and the pain of the other cannot teach, and all who learn from a teacher who doesn't bear the students' burden, who doesn't come to them commanding that they, in turn, bear this burden, cannot learn. All of this requires understanding the nature of the universe itself, the plan of heaven, and a concern for a future that comes embodied in the relationship with an other, rather than a concern merely for the present in which the self is isolated or locked.

Because most people do not understand these things, Rav Simḥa needs to introduce and explain this comment from the Ramban about the manna. Ramban's comment is, for the most part, a recapitulation of a discussion in the Talmud (Yoma 75b), where the nature of the manna is investigated via a verse from Psalms: "Man did eat the bread of the mighty" (Psalms 78:35). Both Rabbi Akiva and Rabbi Yishmael agree that this verse hints that the nature of the manna is not like other foodstuff: Since both humans and angels (the mighty) ate of it, its nature is more transcendent and certainly more mysterious.

The substance of the discussion in the Talmud is that both angels and Israel in the wilderness were sustained by the same source of nourishment: the effulgence of divine light. Rabbi Akiva holds that both the angels and Israel received this sustenance from a shower of light that overflows from the Shekhinah, God's manifestation in the created universe. Rabbi Yishmael, on the other hand, holds that although this is the source of human sustenance, the angels are instead nourished directly from the Divine Height itself, from the Godhead. This is an interesting disagreement between Akiva and Yishmael on the relationship of human beings to God, as compared to the relationship of angels to God. However, as Rav Simḥa writes, regardless of whether one agrees with Rabbi Akiva or with Rabbi Yishmael, the most important point is that it is possible to absorb the divine light into one's being. This light precipitated into a material form, the manna, which was a physical reality that sustained us in our physical state in this world. Furthermore, according to Rav Simḥa, it is still possible for Israel to be thus sustained, to eat the food of infinity in this world. In other words, based on Ramban and the Talmud in Yoma, Rav Simḥa defines contemplation of Torah as the bearing of the burden of the other. The Mussar approach to study is to create what we might call a hermeneutic of deeds, which allows us to engage in the necessary and sustaining contemplation of Torah. This closely resembles Levinas's theory that knowledge itself results from the interpersonal encounter. Levinas insists that ethics is first philosophy, that we begin to explore the world through reason mediated by the encounter with the face of the other. This approach echoes Rav Simḥa's placement of bearing the burden of the other in such a way as to allow for contemplation of Torah to take place. This is not an easy task, but its reward is what we might call, in Levinasian terms, a trace of the infinite in the finite world, represented by the physical incarnation of the divine light in the manna. A desire for the experience of this trace should gird one to persevere in the true contemplation of Torah: the bearing the burden of the other.

In paragraph V, the question of pedagogy was introduced by a talmudic commentary on Psalm 104, which Rav Simḥa called "beautiful and fanciful." We noted that this was not only resonant of the chapter as a whole—entitled "The Sweet and the Beautiful"—but also raised the possibility of hidden meanings in Rav Simḥa's work, especially meanings hidden in this so-called fanciful language. We see that for Rav Simḥa, the special nature of Mussar pedagogy began with a talmudic argument outlining the responsibility of an employer to provide appropriate food to his employees, and the discussion about pedagogy culminates in a talmudic discussion concerning the spiritual nature of food (or, more accurately, the bearing of the burden of the other as the sustaining trace of the infinite in finite form in food). In one context, "food" becomes physical. In the other context, physical "food" is revealed as actually being spiritual. Taken together, this suggests that feeding the hungry in body feeds the soul, while feeding the hungry soul is predicated on feeding the hungry body. This is Mussar.

VIII We see that the letters for "hunger" (רָעָב) and "fire" (בָּעַר) are the same. This is an indication that one should not worry about one's infinite nature, hungering after a spark of this spiritual sustenance. Rather, one should be concerned with fulfilling one's gross materiality. This can only occur because of a lack of proper imaginative projection, but wise people who understands this limitation in themselves will work to remedy it. [For example,] we find concerning our teacher Moses, may he rest in peace, in *Parashat Shemot:* "And when Moses had grown . . ." and "he saw their burdens" (Exodus 2:11). Rashi interprets: "He gave his eyes and heart to be grieved for them"—meaning that he imagined himself (formed in his mind) a mental image. This is even implied by the Torah's choice of language. "He saw" indicates the strength of the mental image as one who imagines a fire and can "feel" the warmth within oneself. In this manner Moses accustomed himself (concentrated on) this mental image, until he could feel their pain as though it were his own. And he immediately bears their burden and feels their burden to outweigh any personal burden he might have had, since theirs is the burden of the many—especially when we talk of the burden of the people Israel: "And all their pain is My pain" (Isaiah 63:9) so that he [Moses] can then speak on behalf of the people, "Why have You dealt ill with this people?" (Exodus 5:22).

What we have referred to as a theme "hidden" in the structure of this chapter becomes more evident as paragraph VIII connects the subjects of hunger and fire—that is, material and spiritual yearning—as two sides of the same coin. Fire, or spiritual light, is precisely the mirror image of hunger. On the one hand, a preoccupation with the hunger implicit in one's own materiality or neediness is an impediment to experiencing this spiritual warmth. On the other hand, learning to bear the burden of the other is the method by which the hunger of self-enclosure is transformed into hunger for spiritual light. When one substitutes the need to feed another physically for the need to feed oneself physically or spiritually, one is truly nourished. However, this is not in any sense easy to achieve, due to the difficulty of learning the skill of proper imaginative projection. This, then, is the heart of the pedagogic problem and serves as the introduction of the pedagogue par excellence (a self-taught or divinely taught pedagogue, at that): Moses our teacher.

Moses can literally create a mental image of the other person's pain and bear it with or for them, and this leads him to discover his own ability to reach the level of prophecy. This intimation of prophecy deriving from the ability to bear the burden of the other will be more clearly stated in the following paragraphs. What we must note at this point, in this introduction of Moses, is that his ability to discern the obligation to love one's neighbor and to translate that imperative into an imaginative projection of the neighbor's pain—the very definition of Mussar that Rav Simḥa is developing—is both definitive of prophecy and within reach, albeit difficult reach, of all human beings. It is this transformation into a "master of a fine soul" that the chapter began with.

Bearing the burden of one person is difficult enough. Moses is shown to be able to bear the burden of the entire people and therefore to stand before God with the burden of the people on his shoulders and speak for them. In fact, Moses is able to bring God into the picture as the bearer of burdens along with him, precisely because as a mere human, he cannot bear the burden of the other entirely by himself.

IX In this regard, how grievous was that which occurred regarding the sin of the "contentious waters" (מֵי מְרִיבָה). The

midrash (Shemot Rabbah, *Va-era* 6:2) says: "At the very hour that the attribute of justice was going to strike Moses, the Holy Blessed One said: 'Withhold from him, because he argues on behalf of the honor of Israel.'" This is what is understood when we say that he gave his eyes and heart to create a mental image of the pain of Israel—as Rashi, may his memory be for a blessing, wrote: "his eyes—this is his rational faculty; his heart—that is, to make his heart one with theirs such that he feels their pain in his heart as though it were his own." As we say: "And you shall *know* this day and turn your heart" (Deuteronomy 4:39)— after he feels the power of his mental image he is very sorry, so to speak, for the pain that the Shekhinah bears on behalf of Israel. In this matter our Sages have said: "When a person suffers, what expression does the Shekhinah use? 'My head is too heavy for Me; My arm is too heavy for Me'" (Sanhedrin 46a).

The ability to bear the burden not only of one other but of many others (namely, Israel) procures for Moses mercy both for Israel and for himself. Bearing the burden of the other is an important mode of achieving *teshuvah,* penitence in its classical formulation. Fundamentally, *teshuvah* is intended to effectively "move" God from the seat of justice to the seat of mercy. Rav Simha uses a comment by Rashi to probe three remarkable connections simultaneously: (1) the connection between head and heart, (2) the connection between human acts of *teshuvah* and, so to speak, divine *teshuvah,* and (3) the connection between human suffering and the divine sensation of that suffering.

Returning to Rashi's comment about Moses' coming to a consciousness of the pain of Israel mentioned in paragraph VIII, Rav Simha emphasizes the explicit connection made there by Rashi between knowledge and empathy. The scriptural verse "And you shall know this day and turn your heart" (Deuteronomy 4:39) functions as a definition: bearing the burden of the other *is* knowing. We might quote Emmanuel Levinas here: "Ethics is an optics." In other words, ethics precedes knowledge, giving direction to rationality so that it leads to knowledge. First we turn toward the other to bear their burden, and only then do we know.

This knowing entails being moved by the pain the Other bears on behalf of others—to be, in Rav Simḥa's language, moved by the divine burden and then to attempt to share the bearing of even this burden. We learn this from a rabbinic saying that states that when a human being suffers, the Shekhinah cries out: "My head is too heavy for Me; My arm is too heavy for Me." The pain of the world is nearly too heavy for even the Divine Countenance to bear. What is remarkable is that Rav Simḥa has already taught us that this is indeed the divine pain that a human being helps to bear, albeit that the human being is Moses.

X We find in the Zohar, *Parashat Mishpatim*: "And they saw . . . a paved work of sapphire and as it were the very heaven for clearness" (Exodus 24:10). We have already written about this, that it requires a great deal of inner wisdom to speak on this. About that which we cannot speak, we can only write. The biblical text must be explained. "A paved work of sapphire"—Rashi explains that this means the memory of Israel's pain. Thus we see how great is the power of doing the commandments in this world—so much so that when the Holy One, so to speak, uses the world of deeds for Israel, God forms an imaginative projection. It is as if God made of the deeds a work of sapphire, to remember the pain of Israel—not, Heaven forbid, that God needs a reminder to remember, but to teach us how great are our deeds in the world. This is similar in to what our Rabbis said: "The Holy One lays *tefillin*" (Berakhot 6a).

Rav Simḥa introduces a biblical image that will illustrate how imaginative projection—the key to a Mussar way of seeing—is also the way God sees. In fact, it is by allowing humans (Moses and the elders of Israel) to also see this way that God became the first Mussar teacher. However, Rav Simḥa is understandably cautious. He must make this point by recourse to classical b texts, which deal with matters about which it is impossible to speak. We are forced to speak of God in human terms and this must be done only with the knowledge that such terms are not to be taken literally.

The biblical passage under discussion reads in full: "Then Moses and Aaron, Nadab and Abihu, and seventy elders of Israel ascended; and they saw the God of Israel; under His feet there was the likeness of a pavement of sapphire, like the very heavens for purity. Yet He did not raise His hand against the leaders of the Israelites; they beheld God and they ate and drank." According to Rashi, this "pavement of sapphire" (i.e., the stonework beneath the feet of God, perhaps supporting the divine throne) is constructed of the memory of Israel's pain. The pain appears translucent: it can be seen through and the view is "the very heavens for purity" or clearness. What is important for Rav Simḥa to establish here is that the world we live in, the world of deeds, constitutes the world for God. It is human activity that God "uses" in seeing the world. God, too, forms an imaginative projection from those deeds. This is the work of sapphire.

Why, Rav Simḥa asks, is this projection made up of the pain of Israel—especially since the deeds that God uses to construct the world are those performed by Israel in obedience to God's commandments, which we would think would produce joy? Rav Simḥa will explore the irremissibility of this–worldly pain even in the acknowledgement of joy in the next paragraph. We cannot, however, leave this paragraph without commenting on the biblical context for this incredible vision that Rav Simḥa is explicating—that is, the climactic point which, following tried and true rabbinic technique, Rav Simḥa does not mention explicitly but assumes that we are aware of. The crucial point is that this "seeing" of the world through the bearing of the burden of the other—a "seeing" that is definitive of both human and divine being—is followed by the act of eating and drinking. As in the previous paragraphs, the spiritual vision is anchored in what we might call the miracle of materiality. This vision of human and divine compassion is not at the expense of flesh and blood obligations. Rather, the God who can bear the burden of creation must allow humans to eat and drink, and in fact must provide the food and drink for them.

> **XI And now we add to this wondrous insight [about the brickwork of sapphire]. A well-known saying of the wise: "Pain and joy are interlaced with one another"—that is, after pain will come joy and the joy will be much greater than if one hadn't experienced the pain before the joy. And now: "When they saw as it were the heaven for clearness," they were already redeemed. Why did the Torah need to add the phrase "a pavement of sapphire" as a memorial to the pain of Israel? Only, it would seem, so to speak, that God had before them the pavement of sapphire in contrast to the very heavens for clearness to raise, as it were, the joy in contrast to this. Obviously, God, the Blessed One, has no need of this. Rather it is to teach God's love for the treasured people and to teach all humanity how important is the obligation of bearing the burden with one's fellow, to be sorry in their sorrow and to rejoice in their joy. And this is a wonder of wonders, that God helps us to understand this wondrous height.**

Rav Simḥa continues to explore this divine imaginative projection in light of a "saying of the wise," reaching "a wondrous insight." The insight addresses the seeming centrality of pain in human life—even human life lived in accordance with the divine commandments.

The answer is, to begin with, that pain and joy are necessarily interlaced. Firstly, this mean that all pleasure includes an element of pain, insofar as the pleasure itself does not fully satisfy us. Moreover, we must recognize that pain is a precursor to pleasure. Pain is what we might call a baseline that allows for the experience of pleasure.

This insight leads Rav Simḥa to ask a remarkable question concerning redemption. Since Moses and the elders were brought up to see God's throne after the redemption from Egypt, why did the Torah refer to the sapphire brickwork, which functioned as a memorial of Israel's pain? What use is pain for a people recently redeemed—who, presumably, still bear the memory of pain close at hand? It was necessary precisely because redemption was not simply the liberation from the slavery, but rather must be understood as bearing the burden of the other—which continues well beyond the physical redemption from Egypt. This idea, which Rav Simḥa calls a great height or high level of understanding, is taught to us by God. Although God has no personal need for sapphire brickwork, it girds the divine throne as an act of loving/teaching, or Mussar—so that we might understand this important lesson.

Thus, to bear the burden of the other leads to redemption and sustains redemption. It also leads to the bearing of the burden of the Other/Creator and it also invokes the Other/Creator to bear the burden of creation itself. This is a creation fashioned out of human deeds, weighed down by pain grounding even its pleasure, but a creation that can be transcended through the bearing of the burden of the other. This, too, is Mussar.

XII   That which we have explained in detail to this point has been explained by our Sages regarding the verse: "Rachel envied her sister" (Genesis 30:1)—the righteous turn the attribute of God's justice to mercy. The meaning of this is as follows. It is written: "The One who fashions unity in His heart, God understands all their deeds" (Psalm 33:15). What is the intent of the word "all"? This is easy: that after God created, God used the deeds of the world in the world, so to speak. Even more so when a person is judged, all of their deeds come before God together—the first deed comes and blesses the second deed. For example, consider the case of people who have wasted time that could have been used to study Torah, who then say that since they are not healthy they are not required to endanger their health in this way. Bring in another of their deeds in this world. Many more arrive and it is clear that there was no hesitation on account of their health. Hence, the second "testifies" about the first, that it was nothing but laziness and their hands are soiled with the transgression of wasting time that could have been used for Torah. Or consider the example of those who do not give charity when it is necessary and say "I am not responsible" (for they are debtors and need to harbor their resources to pay their own debts). They may then bring to them another deed, that they went out to aggrandize themselves and had no such fear. Similarly there are, God forbid, many such acts that they themselves could report, and this is what we mean by "the evil one turns the inclination of mercy to judgment"—that is, their rationalization that they are acting according to the ways of Heaven is disproved by their own deeds and they are punished for both. This is not the case with the righteous. Even when they have an act that might appear to be bad on the surface they bring a higher purpose against this act. For instance, "Rachel envied her sister" appears as though she were guilty of the sin of envy. But the fact that she conquered her jealousy of her sister's righteousness and she passed her husband back to her sister proves that there was no jealousy. The word "jealousy" was used to describe how she felt about all the good deeds of her sister and she thereby transformed a judgment to mercy.

The opposite of imaginative projection is rationalization, which is an important principle in Rav Simḥa's Mussar. Although imaginative projection certainly is an act that depends on the use of the intellect, it is important to recognize that it is not "mere" intellectualization. It is an act shaped by intellectual preparation, by study. However, the use of the intellect, while necessary, is not sufficient. This is a basic tenet of Mussar. The engagement of other faculties beside the intellect formed part of Mussar's attraction to students. This was one of its important differences from other established schools of thought.

In this paragraph, Rav Simḥa describes, in some detail, the ease with which an individual can slip into rationalization. Yet the text that generates the discussion appears to need just such a rationalization for an otherwise inappropriate behavior by one of the Matriarchs. The Bible describes Rachel as having been jealous of her sister, and jealousy is a character trait generally considered to be negative in the Mussar tradition. It is not a trait one would want to use in describing a righteous woman, and the Matriarchs are certainly considered, in the Jewish tradition, to have been righteous.

Rav Simḥa begins by describing what Rachel's act did actually effect: it moved God from the seat of justice to the seat of mercy and it did not occasion any punishment. Many people who act less than righteously think that their rationalizations will likewise cause

God to move from the seat of justice to the seat of mercy, and that they will also be spared punishment for their unrighteous acts. Rav Simḥa goes on to describe the evil that rationalization can mask, and he gives graphic examples of some of its more common forms.

Having learned this important lesson, that God cannot be tricked by rationalization, Rav Simḥa returns to the main problem at hand: Why does Rachel, who seems to have acted unrighteously, receive no punishment? The answer is that through imaginative projection, Rachel uprooted and transformed the trait of jealousy, rather than succumbing to it. Although Rachel is clearly jealous at the beginning of Genesis 30, she eventually comes to realize the pain that she has caused Leah. At that point, she voluntarily turns Jacob back over to Leah, who promptly conceives again. Thus, though the righteous are afflicted by the same evil impulses as we all are, they can transform these impulses into loving deeds through imaginative projection, by bearing the pain that weighs on the other.

In fact, the transformation of character that the righteous accomplish can transform the Divine as well. Righteousness itself is defined not merely in terms of acts, but also in terms of the underlying forces behind such acts, as we saw earlier. Deeds alone do not constitute the world. Rather, the world is constituted by the emotional and intellectual structure of those deeds. Moreover, the Divine Presence, which "creates" the world through human deeds, is moved by the underlying structure of those deeds, and not by the surface rationalizations. Divine knowledge is an ethical optics as much as human knowledge is.

In a remarkable exegetical movement, the "all" of the biblical verse transforms the totality of the "all" into a pluralism. The totality from which the interpretation began ends up opening a non-totalist reading of the structure of reality. This reading, in turn, explains the inherent power of human beings to convert the power of their passions into ethics.

> XIII   In this sad world, this is the most painful fact: There are so many evil qualities that controvert our deeds. For example, even the generally positive trait of honor is sometimes turned this way and sometimes turned that way. How much more so is this true of the accursed quality of envy and, worse still, the very sinful quality of greed. The latter has already been much denounced in the *Sefer Ha-yashar* of Rabbenu Tam of blessed memory, in gate 6, under the subject heading *The 14th Trait, Greed*: "When a person is afflicted with the quality of greed, this evil quality does not come alone but is rather accompanied by other evil qualities. However, the chief evil is that greedy people will not do the commandments until they assess what it will cost them. If it costs them even a small loss they will be lenient regarding it. They will marshal so many rationalizations for this that it has become current to teach that in their own eyes it is impossible for greedy people to transgress. So much do they weaken their heart and eyes, that for a *perutah* they would permit all that is forbidden." Consult that work for further discussion of this matter, but certainly for our purposes we can say that their actions are by definition contradictory. We can also say that those who feel the impulse of this quality must guard their souls well and continually learn Mussar, focusing on texts that address this specific deficiency as well as texts about "bearing the burden." They must come to recognize that the latter is the highest level, as we explained above, and without doubt greedy people cannot achieve this level (God forbid). Therefore one should work very hard to uproot this quality, just as one would uproot actual idolatry.

Rav Simḥa has already established the dangers of rationalization and here he continues to show how deeply pervasive this tendency is. In this he is expounding on the Salanterian notion of "soul roots," those qualities that are embedded in the human soul or psyche which cannot be ameliorated by surface action, but must be uprooted and transformed. The key to this transformation is the study of the appropriate Mussar text (with appropriate passion) and the bearing of the burden of the other. It is the addition of this second part of the prescription that interests us here.

In this penultimate paragraph of the chapter, Rav Simḥa is preparing to return to its key principle: that "ethics is an optics." This will be clearly articulated in the next and final paragraph, which returns to Moses and the brickwork of sapphire. However, Rav Simḥa here demonstrates the connection between this principle and the Mussar of his own teacher. Whereas Salanter showed uncanny insight into the psychological impediments to ethical behavior, Simḥa Zissel incorporates that psychology into a more fundamental epistemology or ontology. However, this exposition is not one in which the existence of individual human beings is founded on that individuality. Rather, it is a "coming into" being by the bearing of the burden of the other; a "coming into" knowledge through the bearing of the burden of the other. Therefore, the psychological techniques of Rav Salanter are effective because they are grounded in an effective analysis of the origin of psychology itself: in the encounter between the self and another.

Tellingly, and profoundly, greed is described as the most counterproductive of character traits because greed is the obsession with oneself that precludes the possibility of bearing the burden of the other. It is the inability to transcend obsession with one's own needs, the inability to substitute desire for another in place of neediness for oneself. Greed is, indeed, the inability to be brought into being by another or to recognize the call of another to oneself; therefore it may be called idolatry. It is this idolatry that Jewish thought, from the Bible onwards, has so passionately fought. In Mussar thought, "You shall have no other gods before Me" is transformed into the functional equivalent of "Love your neighbor as yourself"—that is, love your neighbor *instead* of yourself. This is an act of substitution for another, and this, too, is Mussar.

> **XIV   And we see that Moses our teacher referred to this high quality of bearing the burden in a general way when it says: "And he went out and saw their suffering" (Exodus 2:11). Rashi explains that "he gave his heart and eyes to suffer their pain and therefore went out to see." That means then that the imaginative projection entered his heart. As for the matter of "a work of sapphire," as we wrote: "he went in the way of God"—as it is written, "Why do you strike your fellow?" He was able to do this because his imaginative projections were aligned with God's ways. Therefore he had tremendous compassion on all God's creatures and even more so on God's treasured people, the children of Abraham, Isaac, and Jacob.**

The imaginative projection that accomplishes the transformation of human personality, as Rav Simḥa has already explained, is what propelled Moses out of the complacency of his royal privilege into the violent world of the slave. In this world, by facing and shouldering this world of slavery, Moses learned to view the world through the sapphire brickwork, through the pain of another. However, in this final paragraph of the chapter, the final alignment of human being with divine being comes in the form of a question: "Why do you strike your fellow?"

By adopting this question as his conclusion, Rav Simḥa effectively answers the questions that he raised implicitly toward the beginning of the chapter, in paragraph II: What is the relationship between thought and action in Mussar? Why does ethical action depend on ethical analysis? This answer is that only after allowing oneself to fully enter into the burden of pain of the most oppressed individual, the person most at risk of arbitrary violence, can one then achieve sufficient courage to cry out accusingly: "Why do you strike your fellow?" Without the analysis it is too easy to rationalize. Without uprooting idolatry it is too difficult to substitute oneself for another, too difficult to risk receiving the blows of the oppressor in place of another.

The final stage in Rav Simḥa's system, the goal and result of aligning one's imaginative projections with the Divine Imagination and the concomitant cry against violence, is the emergence of a tremendous sense of compassion for all God's creatures—and especially for God's treasured people, the children of Abraham, Isaac, and Jacob. Why this "more so"? What is the difference between "all God's creatures" and the "children of Abraham, Isaac, and Jacob"? Rav Simḥa is pushing us to consider that at the horizon of our religious imagination, the distinction between "Jew" and "non-Jew" loses its importance. The goal is simply to become a holy human being.

The "more so" of this paragraph is a hint of the surplus of responsibility for Israel, the children of slavery—which, in fact, grounds compassion for all God's creatures. Because of an obsessive concern for Israel enslaved, Moses was able to achieve compassion for all God's creatures. Conversely, the role of Israel in slavery is to provide the basis for human compassion. The memory of Israel's suffering is the memory of the birth: not only of a people in and through slavery, but of the birth of each Jew in and through slavery, and also of the birth of each human in and through slavery. The election of Israel is Israel's memory of this enslavement and the ensuing responsibility in the face of that memory and in the face of every human being similarly enslaved. Each person who asks "Why do you strike your fellow?" is equally elected. The freedom from enslavement requires the concern for the freedom of another. The election of each human being occurs when they take on this responsibility for another, which turns out to be the underlying goal of Mussar—and, for Rav Simḥa, the ultimate meaning of Judaism. When there is no longer any distinction between either Mussar and Judaism, or between a Jew and a human, when the compassion for all God's creatures and more so those oppressed become synonymous, then we can speak of redemption. This "more so" is, then, the heart of Mussar.

Coda

Here I say a concluding "Amen," for our Sages say: "Greater is one who answers 'Amen' than the one who recites the blessing." Why? For this indicates acceptance of the obligation of the words, and therefore I conclude with an acceptance of the obligation of these words. We have learned here that the virtue of bearing the burden of another is very great. It appears that it is higher than, or at least equal to, loving one's neighbor as oneself, because it involves actions, and it is the character trait most essential to general behavior. We have already written: "That which is most difficult reaps the greatest reward." Therefore, to what we have been occupied with in all these talks—to bear the burden with one's fellow—it is well to add this thought: the necessity of accustoming oneself to bearing the burden of another *in practice*. Having described the theory of this virtue, we will now explore the practice—for this is what will give us hope of achieving the blessing of long life and happiness attached to the height of this virtue.

  As we explain the height of the virtue of bearing the burden of another, we will try to understand why all of the great leaders of Israel chose to be shepherds. The reason is that they chose this occupation because of its humble status, and humility leads to compassion. The proud love themselves and the other is nothing to them; they cannot feel the pain of another nor bear the burden with another. Therefore, they [the leaders] accustomed themselves to the role of shepherd, which requires compassion for the sheep and treating them with kindness and gentleness, for this is good for them. If it becomes natural to them to be compassionate toward these creatures of no words, how much more so will they be compassionate toward those who speak. And so the treasured people will learn from this to walk in God's ways, may God be praised.

Now we have the knowledge to clarify precisely the matter of the "brickwork of sapphire" and all that we find that the Holy Blessed One uses, so to speak, in the act of imagining. The matter is thus: All the philosophers agree about the appropriate enlightenment that brings one to immortality. In practice, however, people do not act on the basis such knowledge, but they do so because it is the word of God. This is not surprising, for God is the All in All. However, what we do not often understand is that we cannot replace material goals with spiritual goals. We live in a material world, and this material world will not be impacted by ideas alone but rather by what obligations we accept upon ourselves from Torah. For the focus of the Torah is on the material world: "And all is according to the majority one's deeds [and deeds imply materiality]." Because the structure of existence is more dependent on actions, actions are more holy, as we see in *The Way of Faith* how many material matters contain within them spiritual heights. We thus come to understand that the physical has an inner spiritual core, but in this world it is precisely through doing deeds that the core is made accessible, as it says in

Scripture: "There is no accounting other than deeds."* The Torah itself writes as if God uses the brickwork of sapphire to remember our deeds. And there is nothing new that we bring in this, because God actually speaks in terms of actions. It is obvious that these actions have a spiritual center; for example, *creatio ex nihilo* is important in this regard. In fact, what is new is that deeds have any importance to God. Therefore it is the great honor of the material world to serve as a spiritual place, and more so that the *mitzvot* have a spiritual goal . . . and the words are long.

In his concluding "coda," Rav Simḥa focuses on concerns that I will call both "internal" and "external." By "internal concerns" I mean those of importance to the coherence of his system for the sincere follower of Mussar. By "external concerns" I mean those of importance to the potential student, who is troubled by or otherwise exposed to the thought of the *Haskalah* and its Greek biases. Both the internal and the external concerns are focused on the same basic problem, but they are approached from different perspectives. The problem is that of moving from theory to practice, especially given the importance of theory to practice.

In keeping with the idea of teaching as an ethical act, Rav Simḥa does not begin this discussion as an objective, nonpartisan outsider to the problem under discussion. Rather, by citing the rabbinic teaching about the response "Amen," he acknowledges the need for an act or word beyond the content of teaching itself, a

---

*Although some might argue that Rav Simḥa's translation does no injustice to the biblical author's sentiment, the contextual meaning of this verse in Ecclesiastes seems at odds with how Rav Simḥa understands it. The usual translation is: "Whatever your hand finds to do, do it with your strength, for there is no work, nor calculation, nor knowledge, nor wisdom in Sheol where you are going."

faithfulness to the teaching that implies its acceptance as a weight in one's life. Language itself is an arena for ethical decision-making and requires that one surrender to the obligation that language places one under, as an act of faith. Faith (*emunah*)—saying "Amen"—is not "merely" speaking; it is a speech-act and as such is already a deed. This is what Rav Simḥa wants to teach here. He acts within the narrative itself. And he explains that the content of his acting is to teach that the goal of teaching is not knowledge but rather action. *Ḥokhmah* and Mussar are indivisible. Contemplation *is* compassion.

Contemplation is compassion in real life. This is why one must extend one's Mussar from the academy to the field. One must choose an ethical way of making a living—one that fosters humility and not pride, one that teaches the benefits of caring for others not only in word but also in deed. The paradigmatic occupation for this way of life is that of a shepherd. We learn, in a remarkable reversal, to extend compassion into language from our experience of offering compassion to creatures without language. We learn—as did Abraham, Isaac, Jacob, and Moses—that compassion that begins in the mute caring for speechless creatures comes to us as language in the Torah, as the commandments. And the commandments, in turn, return language to loving deeds.

With this in mind we can identify the flaw in *Haskalah*-thinking, while still being sensitive to its allure. A deep understanding of the profundity of the image of the sapphire brickwork will not only protect us from this temptation, but will also help us to understand that the temptation is so powerful that Scripture itself recognized it and organized itself in such a way as to protect us from it. It is, as Emmanuel Levinas would say, "the temptation of temptations." It is the temptation endemic to all philosophy. All philosophy is, after all, correct *in theory* and can lead us to immortality *in theory*. But immortality *in theory* is absurd. What philosophy cannot do is to command us to act; that command is what we call God's will. An

All greater than the All of philosophy, God's command comes from outside the All of philosophy. God's command refuses to allow us to ignore the physical world. The physical world, the world of people's material needs, is the world of faith for Scripture, for Mussar, for Rav Simḥa. The world of philosophy is disembodied, theoretical, a spirituality that does not understand that spirituality *is* the bearing of the weight of the other. So important is this that God, the ultimate bearer of spirit, enters into language to bring the world into existence precisely out of the nothing of spirit. God then views that world through a material manifestation, the sapphire brickwork, which is at once constructed by human deeds and a reminder of the pain of being human.

Of course, the material world can be said to have a spiritual purpose, but to seek that spiritual purpose removed from the actuality of the material world is, in the end, immoral. Rather, those who try to fulfill the commandments should always keep the spiritual goal of bearing the weight of another in mind. They need to remember that this is their ultimate goal, and not abandon themselves to mere ritualism. But one must also recognize that ascertaining what goal lies beyond that of bearing the weight of another, a more purely spiritual meaning, is beyond us. Rav Simḥa ends by saying that for such an investigation, the "words are long," implying that our time is short.

Chapter Two: Bearing the Burden of the Other

I We have spoken about this bearing the burden of the other many times, and it is not by mere chance that it has been included among the forty-eight statements concerning how Torah is acquired. Its particular characteristic is that it is based

on a combination of the powers of intellect and those of the soul, and one's natural compassion will not succeed in attaining this attribute except by use of the intellect to inscribe the needs of the other onto one's self-contemplation. This we have called to memory in our essay in honor of the Festival of Pesaḥ dealing with the verse "the poor among you" (Exodus 22:24). Despite having taught these principles there, nevertheless it is important to immerse oneself in these matters again here, as we have learned that "the merit of repeating a teaching is understanding" (Berakhot 6b). Both there and here we learn that this is the most inclusive of the attributes. Therefore the prerequisite of Torah for the Torah itself is inclusive of the attributes of the 248 limbs and the 365 sinews of a human being, as is known, and therefore God provides numerous Torah commandments that together should equal the 613 physical elements of a person. These are included in the fifty-eight attributes that accustom a person to using both the power of the intellect and of the soul in acquiring Torah. Since it is the most inclusive attribute, once we reach "bearing the burden" there is nothing beyond, since it includes all of the rest and particularly because it concerns both the body and soul of the other. Therefore we have spoken many times about the beginning of the telling of the life of Moses our teacher, may peace be upon him, that "he saw their suffering." According to the commentary of Rashi, this means that he was prepared to be an agent to relieve Israel's physical suffering at the hands of the Egyptians and then to bring them to worship at the mountain of Adonai, that is Sinai. The Torah thus informs us that one who is worthy of being a messenger to Israel is one who possesses the attribute of "bearing the burden of the other" and whose teaching on this attribute applies both to body and soul.

Rav Simḥa's main point in this paragraph is clear. We have already learned that the supernal Torah cannot be acquired without first having worked our way through the levels of behavior enumerated in chapter 6 of Pirke Avot, culminating in our bearing the burden of our fellow. What we learn here is that learning this lesson requires constant repetition. It must form the core of all learning; the fact that Rav Simḥa has already taught it elsewhere does not prevent him from teaching it again in here. On the contrary: the more we learn, the deeper our understanding may be. Rav Simḥa uses the somewhat unusual formulation of "having called [the subject] to memory [in a previous teaching]," by which he may mean that precisely this teaching will call that teaching to mind. Or, perhaps, he may be indicating that this teaching is never new, but it is always a calling to memory of that fundamental teaching that we have known from the immemorial past.

However, what is of primary concern here, the reason that "bearing the burden" is so central to the acquisition of Torah, is the fact that it requires us to break through the intellect to the world of materiality, and also to train our naturally compassionate impulses through the powers of intellect. Therefore it is analogous to the Torah itself, which requires the commitment of our intellect and the intellectual transformation of our natural tendencies. Rav Simḥa refers to the classical rabbinic formulation that each of the 613 commandments of the Torah corresponds to one of the elements in the human body (Makkot 23b). Thus Torah and the human being are, if not one, then at least inextricably bound together. This makes it more compellingly clear that lifting up the other, another human being, is the equivalent of lifting up the Torah. Further, Rav Simḥa invokes the model of Moses our teacher to suggest that the power of the physical precedes the power of the spiritual. Our own coming to Torah requires a commitment to the material before the spiritual, but more radically, our material is the material of our neighbor. It is not simply that material needs precede spiritual needs, but that the material needs of other people must precede both their own and our own spiritual needs. As Rav Simḥa's teacher, Rav Yisrael of Salant put it, "our neighbor's material needs *are* our spiritual needs."

II   See to what extent the Torah indicates God's preference for addressing the physical needs of others before their spiritual needs. When Jacobs turns to God in prayer he says: "I am not worthy of such kindness and of such truth" (Genesis 32:11). We explain: "of such kindness" refers to Jacob's material needs, and "of such truth" refers to his spiritual needs. This reveals to us that we should emulate this same order of priority regarding others. [Thus the interpretation of this verse appears to me, but the meaning of the phrase "of such truth" is difficult to discern and requires investigation among all the Torah commentators; but in my view this emphasis is correct.]

Likewise we find in the *Ba'al Ha-turim* regarding *Parashat Miketz* on the verse "Before the years of the famine came" (Genesis 41:50). He said: "and to Joseph" is found twice in Scripture, both here and also in "and he said to Joseph, blessed will be the land" (Deuteronomy 33:13). As we have said: all who join in themselves with the community in its pain merit to share in its comfort.

As Rashi wrote, it is forbidden to engage in sexual relations during a famine. We learn that from Joseph, since he had the intelligence to realize this and fulfill his sexual obligations before the onset of the famine so that he would bear the burden of his fellow. This is just like Moses our teacher, may peace be upon him—"and he saw their suffering," even though he grew up in the palace of a king he taught himself to recognize the pain of his fellow. Thus, regarding Joseph, it says "and God hearkened and heard" (Malachi 3:16), indicating that he [Joseph] was remembered before the One who is praised, and he became the king of Egypt, to revive a great nation and smooth the way of Jacob and his sons to enter Egypt with honor rather than in chains, as our Rabbis said. This is what it means to be blessed in the land: that he was an agent for Israel to lead them into the land, to give them eternal life, the pleasantness of eternity in their time.

Go and learn what path one might walk by virtue of bearing the burden of the other and what blessings one will merit.

In this passage Rav Simḥa uses the idea of *imitatio dei* to emphasize that one should be concerned with the material well-being of another before being concerned about one's own spiritual well-being. The Torah tells us that Jacob thanked God for the material benefits he received before thanking God for the spiritual benefits he received then. So, at least according to Rav Simḥa's interpretation of this verse, we should learn to do similarly.

In the course of these comments Rav Simḥa also introduces a theme that he will develop in much more detail below: sovereignty. He refers to Joseph as having become the king of Egypt. As we shall see, the attribute of bearing the burden will, through the introduction of this concept, begin to reveal itself as being variegated and multi-layered. Bearing the burden can produce someone fit to be a king, but everyone who bears the burden is not necessarily a leader.

At the same time, Rav Simḥa's comments here hearken back to a crucial idea expressed in chapter 1—that is, the relationship between Mussar and eternity. The special characteristic of the one who achieves kingship is the ability to "lead the people into the land in blessing." Rav Simḥa correctly reads this phrase eschatologically, but he removes the eschatology from linear chronology. The "pleasantness of eternity in their time" does not look forward to an eternity at the end of days, but rather at an eternity able to interrupt the flow of time, shattering the illusion of time's inevitable passing. In this way, time can be redeemed, as it were, by virtue of bearing the burden of the other.

III   The verse "his father kept the matter in mind" (Genesis 37:11) means that Jacob knew that Joseph possessed an excellence in this attribute. Although he brought an evil report regarding his father and his brothers, this was also for the sake of "bearing the burden of the other," for he worried on behalf of their souls, particularly since they were the founders of the tribes of God, the community of Israel. Thus we find regarding Rabbi Akiva the son of Joseph, that he was lashed several times by the court but he would only respond with more love on that account. [The reason appears to have been that Akiva the son of Joseph, one of those who was martyred, was a reincarnation of the tribes, in order to repair the cosmic damage of their sinfulness—namely, that they had not responded to Joseph's chastisements with love.] And Jacob his father recognized from this that he was obsessively concerned with goodness for the other; therefore, "his father kept the matter in mind." He saw that Joseph was fit for kingship, as we see in the Tosefta: "Just as a king is occupied all his days with the concerns of the community" (Sanhedrin 4:5). That is, it is the nature of a king to be occupied with the concerns of the community, and therefore one who is most diligent in bearing the burden of the other is most fit for kingship. Therefore we are commanded to be careful regarding a king's honor, for he possesses a high level of this attribute of bearing the burden, as we said above. Therefore we are commanded, "One who rebels

against a king is deserving of death" (Joshua 1:18).* The institution of kingship is built on the attribute of bearing the burden beyond comprehension, for in kingship one is responsible
to relieve each individual yoke, as it is said: "On the justice of a
king the land is sustained" (Proverbs 29:4). There is no greater
bearing of the burden of the other than this.

Joseph represents for Rav Simḥa Zissel the prototype of the
messianic king. His fitness for this role is determined by his character, which was already apparent in his youth. Is his role preor-
dained? divinely assigned? hereditary? Rav Simḥa does not supply
us with simple answers. Certainly the chosenness of the Jewish
people is relevant here, and Joseph's innate ability to interpret
dreams similarly reflects a prophetic and unearned power. Joseph
himself will ascribe his interpretive powers to God. And yet,
despite these "supernatural" sources of Joseph's wisdom, it is only
when he unflinchingly undertakes responsibility for his brothers
that Jacob becomes aware of his son's gifts. At the very least, the
portrait of Joseph introduces the related subjects of kingship, on
the one hand, and what we might call the ego's drive for power
and control, on the other. For Rav Simḥa this drive serves (or
should serve) the goal of ethical perfection. Ideally the king, the
political and spiritual leader, is more burdened than other people,
by virtue of his responsibilities for the nation. This is his claim to
kingship. The king's role is to ensure justice in the kingdom, which
requires him to be willing to bear the individual burden of each
individual.

---

*Rav Simḥa "creates" a quote not in the biblical text. We find in Joshua 1:18 that
when the people of Israel accepted his leadership, they said: "Any man who flouts
your commands and does not obey every order you give shall be put to death"
(JPS).

IV   This is what motivated the great ones in Israel like King David and King Solomon, peace be upon them. I did not always understand this, thinking that these righteous ones were simply pursuing honor. Rather, it is because as king one has the possibility of reaching the crown of all the attributes. He must accustom himself to establish a just land, and behold it is in his power to spread wisdom and glorify it—to establish schools and projects to repair the fabric of society. All of this is in the state's power. This is the meaning of the teaching in the Tosefta: "a king is occupied with the needs of the community" (Sanhedrin 4:5)—that is, I think, repairing the social fabric. There is no bearing of the burden greater than this; this is the most inclusive of attributes. Thus David and his son Solomon desired so much to rule, in order to lift the yoke from the whole world. This is the importance of walking in the ways of God, may He be blessed: to establish the condition of the world according to God's way. Therefore one who sits in judgment becomes a partner with the Holy Blessed One in the work of creation.

The smooth functioning of a religious society ultimately depends on the state, which must provide for justice and must collectively bear the burden of the other. For Rav Simḥa Zissel, the symbol of the state is the king. It is for this reason, and not for personal gain or aggrandizement, that the great souls of Jewish history strove for power and its trappings of honor. This teaching of Rav Simḥa's again shows that political matters occupy a major place in his thesis. In our post-Enlightenment world, the social and even physical spaces in which we live are regulated by the state. Therefore, Rabbi Simḥa's approach to corporate responsibility, teaching that the community is responsible for bearing the burden of the other, is particularly relevant. The political leader has the greatest opportunity and the most potential to be the partner of God in the work of redemption. This notion of a divine-human partnership is absolutely fundamental in rabbinic theology. In keeping with his general approach, Rav Simḥa here defines the nature of the human aspect of this partnership: it is to bear the burden of the other. The better able we are to do this by virtue of our status and power in the community, the higher our level of spiritual attainment. To seek political power in order to relieve the burdens of those suffering—and to achieve it—puts us at the level of a David or of a Solomon. Rav Simḥa does not describe a religious quietism. Nor does he choose as religious heroes leaders who are without ego. However, according to his use of these heroic tropes, one may—even must—engage in the world of power politics in order to achieve the ethical world.

> **V, VI, VII This is why our ancestors occupied themselves as shepherds, like Jacob (peace be upon him) and David. Moses our teacher was also a shepherd, because he wanted to accustom himself to bear the burden even of the simple creatures, and all the more so of fellow human beings. We find this midrash (Exodus Rabbah 2:2), which explains that Moses was a shepherd and goes on to teach regarding the verse "God will test the righteous" (Proverbs 30:5):**
>
>> **God tested David with sheep and found that he was a good shepherd. David would bring out the young sheep to pasture [first] in order that they could graze on the best grass. Afterward, he would bring out the old ones in order to give them ordinary grass. Finally, he would bring out the strong ones who could graze on the tough grass. The Holy Blessed One said: "One who knows how to shepherd sheep, each according to its strength, will in the future shepherd My people."**

The Holy One also tested Moses only through his being a shepherd, as our Rabbis said (Genesis Rabbah 2:2):

> When Moses our teacher, peace be upon him, was the shepherd of Jethro, one of My lambs fled and Moses ran after it until it reached a watering hole, where the lamb had stopped to drink. When Moses arrived he said, "I did not know that you fled on account of thirst. You must be tired." He lifted him on his shoulders and walked. The Holy Blessed One said, "You have compassion to treat a lamb in this way—you will become the shepherd of Israel." Thus it is written: "Moses was a shepherd" (Exodus 3:1).
>
> My brothers, gentlemen, understand the wonders of this midrash, which teaches us several great teachings from one word of midrash. Consider the easy things that people scorn, and how people consider these things foolishness. Yet after training themselves in the attribute of bearing the burden, these two great ones assumed the mantle of kingship.

The meticulous concern of the shepherd for his sheep has been elevated to the level of highest spiritual value, and Rav Simḥa now turns his attention to one of the perceived pedagogic problems of Mussar. On the one hand its teachings appear obvious, but on the other hand they require attention to the most commonplace of activities, which seem so easy and obvious that they are taken for granted. Those who seek wisdom and spiritual bliss hunger to be told about the great and unusual tasks that await on the road to either. Attending to the business at hand—such as caring for an innocent animal or child, the small day-to-day responsibilities which constitute the training for attachment to Torah—is scorned as too pedestrian. On the contrary, teaches Rav Simḥa, it was precisely dedication to such responsibilities that prepared David and Moses for kingship, for political leadership now transformed into the highest of spiritual categories.

In these comments, Simḥa Zissel is also subtly addressing what we might call a curricular problem. In the *yeshiva* world that was his milieu, Talmud study constituted the heart of the curriculum, with *halakhah* as its closest rival. Talmud study with the goal of mastering the *halakhah* was the most fervent goal of the *yeshivot* of Simḥa Zissel's day. Midrash, stories devoid of legal content, constituted the "soft" part of the curriculum, and was frequently relegated to the weak-minded. Simḥa Zissel champions the rich spiritual soil of the midrash—and, by extension, the Mussar literature itself.

VIII Moreover, we learn that training in this attribute requires attention to the little things, seemingly of little consequence, which bring one to the most inclusive of all the attributes. It appears to me that this is what the philosophers lack. And further, how beloved in the eyes of God is this training!

Philosophers are especially disdainful of the "little things," according to Rav Simḥa. With their eyes on the "big issue" of essences, they trip, stumbling and kicking, over the "little issue" of ethics, of sustaining the other, their neighbor, the world. Simḥa Zissel's tone is similar to that adopted by the great twentieth-century Jewish philosopher Franz Rosenzweig, who writes in *Understanding the Sick and the Healthy* (as an explanation of his classic *Star of Redemption*):

> Common sense is in disrepute with philosophers. Its usefulness is restricted to the buying of butter, the courtship of a lady, or it may even be of help in determining the guilt of a man accused of stealing. However, to decide what butter and woman and crime "essentially" are, is beyond its scope. This is where the philosopher must enter and assume

"the burden of proof." Such problems are beyond the reach of common sense. *These are the "highest" problems, the "ultimate" questions.* (emphasis added)

IX,X   We learn moreover that one needs to continue one's training throughout one's life, as Scripture teaches: "Train a child . . . and even when he grows old" (Proverbs 22:6). Our words on this matter are well known. Go out and see how these two great men, Moses and David, occupied themselves in training in light of our interpretation.

Moreover, we have revealed that these things, in which one should constantly train oneself, are easy—easy but not insignificant. They are, in fact, the essence of religious knowledge, as the Sages say: "From where do we know that rabbis are called kings?" (Gittin 72a). That is, the Torah scholars of the earlier generations were students of the attribute of bearing the burden of the other—to establish as a reality the divine plan, and this was called kingship. The blessing we pronounce on seeing a king is "that God gave honor to human beings," indicating that God gave the king the strength in the external world of revealed deeds to establish God's plans.

Rav Simḥa's pedagogy has emerged in more detail in this second chapter. In chapter 1, the radical nature of Mussar occupied center stage. Mussar is the acquisition of Torah, the interruption of the finite world by the infinite as the burden of the other. Mussar is the optic through which God views the world, the suffering of human beings that obligates us to respond. But despite its radical nature, Mussar is located in small gestures, in the unassuming but obvious demands of life. It is, to paraphrase the Torah itself, "not so far off" that we should relegate its actualization to philosophers. Rather it is nearby—"in our mouths" (Deuteronomy 30:14). Paradoxically, this makes Mussar all the more in need of constant awareness, of *ḥinnukh*—which I have translated consistently as "training" (rather than the more common renderings "education" or "teaching"). This translation captures more faithfully both the nuance of attention to the "easy" things that Rav Simḥa emphasizes, and it also avoids the more generalized, more abstract sense of "education." For Rav Simḥa, pedagogy is divided into two interconnected spheres: Talmud and Mussar. The first is a contemplative study of Jewish sacred texts, while the second is an affective moral training that breaks through the deceptive traps of education in order to transform the individual from materiality to spirituality. The spirituality, the acquisition of Torah, is accomplished by our lifting the burdens of material life off of our neighbor.

In these two paragraphs Rav Simḥa reiterates the need for reiteration. Although the point he has made throughout this text is both simple and clear, it bears repeating over and over, as an example of how the simple and clear insights of Mussar must be an integral part of a continuous and ongoing training. Further, for the first time he states explicitly that earlier rabbis were concerned with this very Torah and Mussar, which is expressed by bearing the burden of the other. Rav Simḥa also makes the relationship between rabbi and king explicit: they become synonymous. We might suggest that in contradistinction to the platonic ideal of a philosopher/king, Rav Simḥa offers us the rabbi/king or king/rabbi—the ideal political leader defined by the justice of his deeds. Those deeds, acts of bearing the burden of the other, are further defined precisely as revelation. God is revealed in the world not by word but by deeds, our deeds.

> **XI,XII** **What they said about this principle rests on this statement: "Greater is service *[shimmush]* of Torah than its learning *[limmud]*" (Berakhot 7b). That is, one becomes a complete Torah scholar, bearing the burden of one's fellow and sustain-**

ing the world, through service of accustoming oneself to bear the burden, and also by a love of Torah. This is the most inclusive of all the attributes.

Joshua therefore merited kingship, for he did not move from the tent of his service. This is in keeping with what Rashi of blessed memory commented [to Numbers 27:16–21], that Moses our teacher had requested the kingship for his own son. The Holy Blessed One said to him: "Better is the service of Joshua, that he should be king." This is because he [Joshua] accustomed himself to bear the burden of the other more [than did Moses' own son]. And it is like the midrash above, concerning the two great ones Moses and David.

The chapter concludes with an interpretation based on a linguistic insight. Rav Simḥa focuses on a relatively obscure talmudic statement about *shimmush torah,* service of Torah. This is by no means seen as a classical Jewish value–concept, but Rav Simḥa nevertheless uses it to replace the central rabbinic value concept of *talmud torah,* study of Torah. The true *talmid ḥakham,* or rabbinic sage, is not merely a learner of Torah, a *lomed torah,* but rather a servant of others because of Torah, a *meshammesh torah.* Love of Torah is love of others; it is bearing the burden of others. And this sustains the world. Rav Simḥa points to the fact that Joshua succeeded Moses as rabbi/king of Israel because he was a greater servant than Moses' own son. This is the power of Mussar.

Chapter Three: The Order of Redemption in Egypt

I The Torah prefaces the "vision of the bush" story with a complete genealogy of Moshe our teacher, may peace be upon him. The Torah says that "Moses grew up" (Exodus 2:11), which

Rashi explains means "to greatness, since Pharaoh appointed
him over his house." It was thus ordained for him to become
connected to Pharaoh. That same verse continues, "he went out
to his kinsfolk and witnessed their labors." Rashi explains: "He
placed his eyes and heart to feel their suffering." That is to say,
Moses always perceived by means of his visceral sense, for this
sense is more effective than hearing about events (secondhand).
As a result, one who always perceives in this way becomes a
"bearer of the other's burdens." It is as if he himself is actually
bearing their burdens. This is in keeping with the meaning of
Avot, chapter 6: to "bear the burden of one's fellow" is to dili-
gently seek the benefit of the other in every possible way.

Rav Simḥa begins this section with exegetical questions: Why
do we not first meet Moses at his encounter with God at the
burning bush? What do we learn from the fact that the Torah provides a biography for Moses? The answer addresses precisely what
it was that made Moses worthy of the encounter at the burning
bush: his obsessive preoccupation with bearing the burden of the
other. This trait is what made Moses worthy to receive divine
communication, and it also explains why he attained the stature of
rabbi/king and eventually became a model of righteousness for
time to come. How Moses developed this trait, this preoccupation
with the burden of the other, is clear from the biblical text. The
circumstances of Moses's birth and upbringing connected him to
Pharaoh, signaling that he was somehow mysteriously chosen for
greatness. Despite his privileged position, Moses' intuitive response
was to "go out"; he was inextricably drawn by the suffering of the
Hebrews and he made them his people by going out to actually
see and feel their suffering. Neither the Torah nor Rashi explains
how this happens. Rav Simḥa, however, asserts that it is by way of
the imaginative projection we have already discussed, but here the

projection is described as a visceral projection. Moses puts himself in harm's way. And this putting of himself in harm's way, of standing between the oppressed and the oppressor, is another trait, along with obsessive preoccupation, that defines Moses' greatness.

II   Later in that verse, the Torah tells that [Moses'] "bearing the burden" [applies] not only to the masses, but to individuals as well: "and he saw an Egyptian man beating a Hebrew, one of his kinsmen" (Exodus 2:11). The Torah is precise [to show] that he had [a sense] of brotherly love for this individual. Afterward the Torah tells us that one should save the oppressed from his oppressor not only when an Egyptian strikes a Hebrew, but also when "two Hebrews are fighting, and he said to the offender, 'Why are you hitting your fellow?'" (Exodus 2:13). Thus, this principle of bearing the burden of one's fellow also applies to one who is oppressed by a Hebrew: one should also want to save such a person from oppression.

Obsessive preoccupation with the suffering of the other person is explicitly *not* to be understood in terms of generalities. It is not enough to be concerned with the suffering masses in the aggregate or even to bear the burden of such a group. Rather, suffering occurs one person at a time, and must therefore be borne one person at a time. Neither is it sufficient to bear the burden of the suffering of one's own people at the hand of foreign oppressors. The suffering that can be inflicted by one's own family, friends, or people is equal reason for such an obsessive preoccupation.

III   Later the Torah tells us that he did not just dwell quietly and calmly in this region, in the land of his birth, but rather in a different land, Midian. He lived in a foreign land, fleeing from Pharaoh and from death. Surely he was wandering and

distracted by his own sorrows. Nevertheless, when he saw what the shepherds did to the daughters of Midian, driving them off unjustly, "Moses rose to their defense" (Exodus 2:17), even in the land of his estrangement while fleeing death himself. Moses was among the "haters of ill-gotten gain," and this refers to the burden. This is how Ramban, may his memory be blessed, explains it in *Parashat Yitro*: Here too [referring to Jethro's instruction to Moses to appoint "men of courage, those who fear Adonai" (Exodus 18:21)], "Moses rose to save them." And Scripture says further that he did not only save the daughters of Midian from their oppressors, but he also "watered their flocks."

The trait of putting himself in harm's way, combined with an obsessive preoccupation with the suffering of another, is further emphasized by Moses' maintaining these traits even in flight, even in exile. Whereas the rational person would be concerned only with their own safety, Moses acted beyond such reason. In Midian, Moses cannot abide the idea that the shepherds who are taking advantage of Jethro's daughters will profit and will become the bearers of ill-gotten gain. But justice is not Moses' only motivation. Moses does not stop after preventing an act of injustice, but goes on to water their flock. He goes beyond the letter of the law, and even beyond that. He is guided by an excessive insistence for the good. His is a messianic obsession, befitting a deliverer.

Taken together, these opening paragraphs of chapter 3 describe the impossible goal of saintliness in its paradoxical possibility. This saintliness or righteousness may be considered a messianic vision for which we aim. It is never quite attainable but we know that it has been attained in the past. Redemption is not a future speculation, but rather a past and future fact. The centrality of the exodus and Moses' personal story are both crucial to any interpretation of

Judaism, but they are especially central to Mussar. It is essential in Mussar to know that we cannot be Moses, and yet equally essential to know that we *may* be Moses. In our own exile and in the distraction of our own flights and pain, the possibility of excessive obsession with the suffering of another is an ever-present critique of our slumber.

IV **And later we deal with an issue of practical importance. In** *Parashat Shemot* **it states: "(Then) Moses and Aaron went and assembled all the elders of the Israelites . . . and the people believed. When they heard that God had taken note (of the Israelites) . . ." (Exodus 4:29–5:1). And later it is written: "Afterward Moses and Aaron went to Pharaoh and said to him, 'Thus says the Lord, the God of Israel: Let my people go . . .'" (Exodus 5:1).**

We are being quite precise (in examining these verses), for it seems as though it would have been better if they [Moses and Aaron] had gone to Pharaoh first, and afterwards reported back good news to Israel, that they had been with Pharaoh and he had said to him: "Let my people go!" After all, they came to Pharaoh, the mighty king, without permission. Considering that Moses had a death sentence with Pharaoh, how could Pharaoh have allowed him to live—especially since this request was a revolt against the king, for there is no greater rebellion against the monarchy than saying: "Make us a free people!" And there is no greater revealed miracle than this. Since this would have brought great comfort to Israel, why does the gathering of the people of Israel come first? It is because one is not worthy of redemption without having faith. This revealed miracle would not have happened to them if they had gone to Pharaoh [first]. Therefore, let this be known to Israel first, writing: "And the people believed when they

heard that God had taken note . . ." (Exodus 4:31). Therefore, immediately after it is written: "Afterward" (Exodus 5:1), meaning that only after they believed "did [Moses and Aaron] go to Pharaoh." Were it not for [the people's] faith, [Moses and Aaron] would not have been able to go to [Pharaoh], particularly to say: "Let My people go." Only after faith were they able to rebel against him; otherwise they would not have been able to do anything.

This paragraph might come, at first, as a surprise. Until this point, Rav Simha has focused his remarks on the supremacy of action in Jewish religious life. He has taken religious observance and belief for granted without examining it. In particular, he has stressed the near-cosmic importance of the characteristic of bearing the burden of another, which is definitely related to action. Yet, in this paragraph Rav Simha does exactly the opposite, asserting the priority of faith to action. This should neither be surprising nor confusing. On the contrary, it is an essential moment in the discovery of Mussar. Bearing of the burden of another is not and cannot be motivated by reason alone. The imperative to act for the other devolves upon us from some source that is not susceptible to the analysis of reason. The faith that Rav Simha is describing is not a faith defined by a creed or a set of propositions. (After all, the Torah itself had not yet been given at this point in the biblical narrative.) Rather, this faith is almost concurrent with the bearing of the burden that he describes.

The people of Israel should not, logically speaking, have assented to Moses' mission to Pharaoh. To rebel against a king means to break all bonds of civil behavior. This is true even when the rebellion is done by slaves, for even slaves are indeed part of the community. They have a role in society and they are taught to accept that role both through the rational understanding of the polity and through oppression. In fact, the rational understanding of the polity and oppression is often the first act of violence to which we all as individuals must acquiesce—that is, in order to live together in a political structure, the individual must already acquiesce to a level of obligation imposed against our will. Incredible inertia is required to confront the overwhelming structure of the oppression. The violence involved in such an act may sometimes be only implicit or psychological, rather than physical, but it is violence nonetheless. In the face of this overwhelming pressure, Moses and Aaron act as bearers of the burden and they break through the accepted political structures of their society. They are able to present the people with a different paradigm, one that invokes the memory of the God who is outside the people's conventional analysis. This memorial of God is precisely contained in the example of Moses' and Aaron's bearing of the burden and in their command to the people to accept this new paradigm, in which they must take on responsibility for the suffering of their compatriots. Their struggle with this new paradigm will characterize the people's struggle to reach spiritual maturity throughout the wandering in the wilderness; however, with this faith, Moses' mission becomes possible.

V   When we examine God's commands closely, we see precisely this order. From the beginning, the Holy Blessed One told Moses of the polarity of his mission. The first aspect of the mission needed him particularly: "Come, I will send *you* to Pharaoh, and *you* shall free My people . . ." (Exodus 3:11). The second aspect of the mission did not need him. Later God told him what to say to Israel: "The God of your ancestors has sent me to you" (Exodus 3:15). By this, God will come to Israel to bring them news of redemption. And later . . . God explained how it would happen, for it was precisely in this order that they were redeemed: "Go and assemble the elders of Israel and say to them: Adonai, the God of your ancestors . . . has appeared [to me and said]: I have taken note . . ." (Exodus 3:16), and after this it states: "They will listen to you" (Exodus 3:18), which means that they will believe. Rashi explains, "For they already had this sign . . . that by the very expression of this phrase they are redeemed." Therefore, they will believe in you, and once they have this quality of faith, it is immediately afterwards that "you shall go . . . to the king of Egypt and say to him" (Exodus 3:18). It was according to this order that Moses and Aaron did the following: "They assembled all the elders of the Israelites . . . and the people believed . . . afterward Moses and Aaron went" (Exodus 4:29–5:1)—to redeem them.

Rav Simḥa extends his discussion of this section in the Torah, continuing to draw inferences from the narrative sequence to support his teachings about Mussar. We learn that there is a dual aspect to the quality of redemption. Redemption "elects" the individual who bears the burden of another, and redemption is also transmitted to the larger community through "faith"—that is, the memorial of a past that breaks through the analyses of reason in the present. Rav Simḥa again relies heavily on reading Rashi's commentary, here quoting Rashi on the verse "They will listen to you." Rashi says that they will listen to Moses because they have already had this sign: "by the very expression of this phrase they are redeemed." Rav Simḥa uses Rashi's comment here to emphasize that language itself is the sign of the redemption of Israel. God is concerned for Israel, and that concern is expressed in God's voice and also through Moses' taking on the burden of another. These two elements combine to make the redemption as if it had already occurred. This idea is thematically connected with the opening paragraphs of chapter 1, which stress that eternal life and this-worldly life are a series of interruptions one inside the other, and not simply a linear progression. Redemption is here seen as the equivalent of eternal life, and it too interrupts the non-redeemed world rather than following it in linear fashion.

> **VI   This is our order of redemption: bearing the burden; as it were, the One who sends a message from the bush; the messenger and his preparation; and, finally, the quality of faith and then redemption. Behold the redemption from Egypt is a sign for future redemption—may we be privileged to prepare ourselves according to this order—and let it be food for us in this world and the next. Amen, and so may it be God's will.**

Finally, Rav Simḥa summarizes the argument that he has been developing throughout this chapter. Redemption proceeds along a continuum. First an individual must step forward to bear the burden of another. Then, if that person is well enough prepared spiritually, God communicates miraculously with them. Then faith follows and redemption depends upon this faith. Rav Simḥa also invokes the oft-repeated rabbinic idea that the Egyptian redemption story is the prototype of the future redemption of the Jewish people and of the world.

Chapter Four: Bearing the Burden of the Other's Pain: A Boundless Imperative

> **I   Someone once suggested to me that one ought to be glad and grateful just for being in a modestly good state of health. I thereupon shared with that person the following awe-inspiring sermon:**

I acknowledge your appreciation and regard for God's gestures of kindness. Fine, but take notice of how we are prone to exhibit misjudgment in this matter. When we observe a satisfactory medical improvement in someone who had been ill, we are wont to rejoice and lay aside all empathy. This impulse is premature, for so long as the other is not experiencing a total recovery, we ought to still share the burden of their physical and emotional discomfort. Indeed, for the person who is in the process of recovering, anything short of a total recovery is, at least in some measure, a source of physical pain and emotional agony. Thus, one should share the yoke of the other's discomfort, even if they are only slightly short of a comprehensive and total recovery. Indeed, we lose sight of the other's pain when their discomfort is not dramatic. Therefore, when we learn about the other's improved medical condition—namely, that they are now in a modestly good state of health—we tend to feel relieved and lay aside all empathy.

One who properly takes on the yoke of the other's pain, however, is not tempted by this commonplace impulse. They impress upon their own soul the pain and agony of the other. Acting not merely on instinctive sensibilities, one thus brings oneself to share (and, ultimately, to bear the burden of) the pain of the person experiencing the incomplete recovery.

This paragraph is a perfect example of the dangers of sleep and the spiritual height of what we've called wakefulness. When a person has been ill and then begins to recover, most of us relinquish the pain we might have felt on their behalf during their illness. The more fully they recover the more this is true. Yet, the person who has been ill continues to be pained by their diminished health, despite the *relative* improvement in their status. The importance of being sensitive to such situations cannot be overstated. More importantly, however, Rav Simḥa characterizes the initial empathy we feel for the sick person as an instinctive sensibility. One does not require training in Mussar to be empathetic to someone in the throes of pain. However, empathy is not enough. It is fleeting. It does not flow from the depths of love. Empathy is an emotion that distances us, even as it allows us to think we are bearing the burden of another. In empathy, we cannot help but be aware that the other's pain is not our own. However much we may feel badly for our neighbor, we simultaneously feel relieved that it is another's pain and not our own. This feeling is precisely the opposite of bearing the burden. One who truly bears the burden, one who is a true lover to the beloved who is stricken, cannot abide even a modicum of the beloved's pain. He is obsessed with relieving all of the pain, however little of it remains, for as long as the illness persists. Thus, bearing the burden is not an instinctive sensibility. The instinctual sensibility—empathy, in this case—is a way of returning to sleep. The wakefulness of Mussar requires the transformation or transcendence of the natural instinct into something else . . . into love. The infinite demand can only be engaged by an infinite responsibility, a messianic responsibility, which is here described in the context of everyday human situations.

II The biblical narrative [Genesis 24] supports this claim: Rebecca made an effort to extend kindness, even though the discomfort to be alleviated was minimal. She herself drew the water for the camels, to save the servants of Eliezer from troubling themselves with this task. Consider how infinitesimal their discomfort would have been had they drawn the water themselves. And consider, now, how the course of events that

followed would have been different, had she not done this small act of kindness: Rebecca would not have become the daughter-in-law of our ancestral father Abraham; nor the wife of our ancestral father Isaac; nor the mother of our ancestral father Jacob. Nor would she have become a matriarch of the Israelites.

Take notice of what rewards accrue to a bearer of the other's immeasurably minimal pain. Now imagine [the loss] when the other's pain that we fail to bear, Heaven forbid, is more than minimal. Consider how much one can gain for so little, and how for so little one can lose so much. How frightful! How awe-inspiring it is to reflect upon the merit of bearing the burden of the other's pain in the spirit of Mussar.

Once again Rav Simḥa returns to the theme of the importance of the extraordinary within the ordinary. He also returns to his role as commentator on the Torah, turning to the story of Rebecca at the well. In this story, Rav Simḥa points out, the need that Rebecca responded to was essentially trivial. It would have taken very little effort for Eliezer's servants to draw water for their camels on their own. Eliezer's request of Rebecca was simply that she share her water with him. But Rebecca is obsessed by this request. She cannot do enough for Eliezer and his retinue; their slightest need becomes the source of her pleasure. Rav Simḥa is not necessarily suggesting that we can each become a Rebecca, or even that we *should* strive to do so. However, he suggests that if Rebecca's reward for bearing a minimal burden was so extraordinary, then we probably never fully realize the complete consequences of the good we do. Moreover, most of us are presented with far less minimal burdens to bear than Rebecca was, and if we fail to bear them the consequences may, indeed, be grave.

This Mussar message Rav Simḥa lauds may also be expressed

in terms of the idea of excess. The obsessive undertaking of bearing the burden of the other, which is a sine qua non of Mussar sensibility, may perhaps strikes us as excessive. However, it is precisely the excessive nature of the good, its "unreasonableness," which frees it of the limits to which our logic would otherwise subject it. If we do that which is reasonable, we have not yet done that which is good. Generally, when we do that which is reasonable, our reason warns us against accepting the yoke that doing good necessarily becomes. It is, in fact, our reason that encourages us to sleep in the presence of suffering. However, suffering is also an excessive entity. It also is outside the boundaries of our logic and "does not make sense." If logic constrains our impetus to do that which is good, what logic constrains suffering, or evil? Our experience suggests that no such constraint exists. Unless suffering calls to us, unless it mobilizes us to act against it on another's behalf, it is unconstrained and becomes ubiquitous.

Chapter Five: Whosoever Lacks Proper Manners Is Alien to the Organism of a Civilization

I From your letter, which I received today, one learns that our dear friend . . . has journeyed to Jaffa to study in isolation. I hasten and do not tarry to write back to you today, as you shall transmit to him on my behalf that he acted on a serious misjudgment; it is beyond comprehension that one would act on such a decision without having first conferred with me. Indeed, he did write to me on a number of occasions that the Mussar lectures do comfort his soul, as they breathe in him a living spirit. And this must truly have been the case, as these lectures espouse the living word of God. How, then, did it become possible that he cast behind him a place of living

waters? How is it that he does not take into consideration that this misdeed might well be the subject of the verse: "'And that which is wanting cannot be numbered' (Ecclesiastes 1:15)— that refers to one whose comrades wish to include him in a religious act, but he excludes himself" (Berakhot 26a)?

Rav Simḥa is reacting here to the defection of one of his disciples. Specifically, it seems, this particular student has left the Mussar community in Lithuania and instead opted for a life of religious isolation, presumably among the pietists of the Land of Israel. This letter throws some light on the social-religious tensions of the time, if one assumes that the student has joined the *Hovevei Tziyon,* the earlier religious pioneers who are generally considered the forerunners of modern Zionism. The letter also raises the larger issue of how important it is to have a strong, supportive community to help achieve religious goals. This, in turn, brings up the issue of isolation versus community as a religious ideal, and it is on this level that Rav Simḥa will continue. A student who has "cast behind him a place of living waters" has made a grievous mistake. But as we will see below, the mistake stems from the fact that the student has ignored his responsibility to the others in the community, to bear their burden.

II Know that it would be unthinkable to experiment with this eccentric religious practice—that is, to act without grounded and responsible deliberation—unless one lacked an appreciation for the doctrine of bearing the burden of the other's pain. If one is receptive to this religious-ethical principle (highlighted by our Sages of blessed memory, in but these few short words) and if one meditates upon it and comes to fully appreciate its awesome centrality to the Jewish religious experience, one will likewise appreciate that this principle points to the veracity of our revealed tradition. This person will, furthermore, appreciate that our Sages of blessed memory regarded this principle as a means by which to acquire Torah. After all, why is this trait so bound up with the acquisition of Torah? But a discerning spirit understands that the two—bearing the burden and acquiring Torah—are closely connected; indeed, they are one and the same. For we will likewise concede that one who cannot appreciate this code of practice is inherently and positively alien to the organism of a civilization—indeed, boorish.

Boorishness is an expression of stunted egoism. The boor is one who never develops past the point of satisfying one's own needs, never developing the desire for another person and the concern for the needs of another that marks the truly religious individual. Only by surpassing boorishness is it possible to experience empirically, through the truth of life, the truth of revelation. The experience of the individual whose bearing the burden of another acquires Torah can, in a manner of speaking, serve to authenticate revelation. To experiment with "eccentric practices," to withdraw from the responsibilities of bearing the burden of the other in favor of a self-satisfying religious quest, renders the student a boor in this sense of the word.

III   Indeed, all of the philosophers have considered humankind a social animal, insofar as the world functions and survives on the basis of a social contract. And why were we created in this manner? Could not the Creator of the world have created us differently, God forbid, so that we would not need each other? But God wants us to discern that we are to be concerned with the other's spiritual welfare, just as we are concerned with our own. Yet, because the human being by inclination is more intimately sensitive to material matters than to spiritual ones, it is with the former that the Creator fosters this ethic. God thus

ordained that one's material pursuits be inescapably entwined
with the material pursuits of others. Consider, for example, the
agronomist, whose aim is to cultivate crops for the multitudes
that inhabit the world, thus gaining access to all of the other
necessities of life, such as clothing. Or consider the merchant,
who travels afar to bring back merchandise (such as garments)—and by extension servicing himself, as explicated
above. The same can be illustrated in every other domain of life.
One who is reflective will, by way of one's material pursuits,
infer that this interplay exists even more so in spiritual matters
than in material ones—namely, that one's spiritual welfare is
inextricably entwined with the spiritual welfare of others.

Human need as expressed in our material nature is the sine
qua non of creation. It may even be considered the rationale
for creation itself, for creation is, by definition, an ethical phenomenon. The ability of human beings to achieve a spiritual
nature on the same par as that of the Creator depends on our
ability to accept an ethics. This is the single characteristic that we
can discern of the Divine, in the midst of the otherwise mysterious character of what is beyond the ken of human consciousness.
Were we not material, says Rav Simḥa, we could not be or
become spiritual. To become spiritual is to bear the burden of
another, just as God is presented as bearing the burden of creation. In order to move toward this spiritual goal, we must
become aware of the interdependent burdens of our materiality, so
that serving our own good will always coincide with assuring the
good of another.

The model of economic life in society can serve as a model to
our spiritual search. Those who produce any kind of material
goods can only ensure their own well-being by simultaneously
providing for the well-being of others. So too on the interpersonal

level, we are instructed that one can only serve one's own well-being by providing for the well-being of others.

> **IV   God, the blessed One, unceasingly seeks the good of humankind, and wished to bestow upon humanity a favorable share of everything the world has to offer. It is out of sheer graciousness that God ordained that we attend to our material needs in this manner, so that we would thus be led to infer that spiritual matters might also be attended to precisely by way of attending to the other. Therefore: whoever does not attend to the needs of another is effectively not attending to their own needs, as explicated above.**

This is God's grace: that we are materially interdependent and that interdependence reveals to us the interdependence of our spiritualities as well.

> **V   The above resonates agreeably with the rabbinic assertion that "whosoever lacks proper manners is alien to civilization." One who is ignorant of the way of the world—i.e., that humans are ordained to act on the exigencies of a social-political-economic structure where "giving is getting"—must be also foolishly unaware of the essence of our humanity. This being the case, such people ought to be forbidden from living among people, as they are a danger to society. This is also reflected in the wise words of the *Migdal Oz*, under the entry *derekh eretz*: "Whosoever lacks proper manners lacks the mark of a human being, and is comparable merely to the beast of the wilderness, as in the verse: 'When a wild horse's colt is born a human being'" (Job 11:12).**

What we call "manners" in English, and what we mean by "manners" in American society, differs in important respects from the sense of the term *derekh eretz* in Hebrew and its meaning in Jewish culture. The Hebrew term certainly includes the areas of common etiquette subsumed under "manners," and the importance of such common courtesies cannot be overstated. However, *derekh eretz* (literally, "the way of the land") also refers to what we would call civic responsibilities. A person who has *derekh eretz* is a good citizen, one who realizes that actions in every sphere of life—economic, political, social, and cultural—all have an impact on others, either for good or for ill. Beyond this realization, of course, looms the responsibility for the other that Rav Simḥa has already emphatically taught us. Thus, our social, political, and economic decisions should not be guided merely by the fact that they impact others. Rather, they should grow from the realization that we can control that impact so as to maximize the good of others. To the extent that this is possible, it is required of us.

The understanding of *derekh eretz* as civic responsibility, however, should in no way diminish our understanding of it as manners also. The simple acts of common courtesy are often the simple, everyday occasions for our potential to bear the burden of another. Manners are the most common ethical acts we can perform, and taking them lightly establishes a pattern of behavior that can have significant consequences on a larger scale. Emmanuel Levinas, was fond of saying that "After you," the too-often rote intonation of placing another before us, precisely summarizes all of the great ethical principles of all the philosophers. Rav Simḥa clearly would have agreed.

VI Let us please think through the following. Had Abraham our forefather, of blessed memory, not concerned himself with the dissemination of monotheism—how woeful, had this come upon us!—we would be stripped, Heaven forbid, both of a temporal and an otherworldly existence! And had Moses our

teacher, of blessed memory, not constricted his soul (as relayed to us by the Rabbis, of blessed memory in *Mekhilta, Beshallaḥ*) when he ascended on high to obtain the Torah, from where else would we acquired it? How else would we know how to establish a civilized world, and what the principles of proper conduct are?

[Scripture] has established a world of intelligence out of which developed a civilized organism and thus a socio-economic scheme that survives on one's bearing the burden of another. We are compelled to infer that with spiritual growth this is so much more the case: nurturing the other's spirituality is part and parcel of the experience and of the efficacy of the pursuit toward personal spiritual growth. After all, is it not the case that our murky carnality is purified by the soul, as it assumes a spiritual existence on the merits of its interaction with the soul?

Earlier in this chapter Rav Simḥa mentioned the social contract theory of ethics. He suggested that secular philosophers adopt the model of the social contract in order to explain why human beings need to be concerned about one another. Here, however, Rav Simḥa reveals that he considers the social contract theory to be inadequate. It does show that even secular philosophers stumble their way toward the notion of bearing the burden of another, but it does not account for the intrinsic goodness toward which the human being strives, on the journey from mere existence to existence as a soul. To account for this more profound and radical understanding of human consciousness, we must move beyond the social contract and consider the experiences of two particular human beings: Abraham our forefather and Moses our teacher and lawgiver.

Rav Simḥa has already dealt with Moses and other biblical figures, so his understanding of their experience should not be surprising to us. Both Moses and Abraham are human beings who are transformed by the experience of bearing the burden of others. It is their experience that precipitates what we more commonly call their faith. The certainty of their faith is what compels them to make known to others what they have learned. We have already seen that teaching is a primary Mussar value. Abraham learns the truth of monotheism. It is this truth upon which the edifice of human ethics must stand, for monotheism is nothing other than the full realization of the impossibility of shirking or avoiding our responsibility for the other. The philosophic or theological doctrine of monotheism is only a pale expression of the experience of the unimpeachable otherness of my neighbor, my beloved. It is this stance vis-à-vis another that constitutes the core of the experience that will be called monotheism. Without this commanding experience, there is no warrant for our behavior.

Thus, monotheism requires the idea of command. As soon as we fully recognize the inability to become one with the other, our stance toward that other is transformed: they now stand above us, commanding our loving response. The translation of this command into the details of economic and social life is credited to Moses. The transformation of carnality—that is, our sheer materialism—into soul is accomplished by the combined efforts of these two related phenomena: monotheism and commanded-ness.

VII Be assured that it is my wish to expand greatly on our discussion. But writing physically drains me—may this not befall you! (*lo aleikhem*, spelling *aleikhem* with an *alef* and not with an *ayin*, as most people spell it).

Significantly, in contrast to *aleikhem* with an *ayin*, *aleikhem* with an *alef* addresses a broad scope of social affinities. Notice again how far-reaching the mandate to bear the burden of another's pain is—as "another," in the broadest sense of the term, extends to another's family, friends, and acquaintances and, as such, one must include them in one's concern.

This expression [*lo aleikhem*, "not to you"] appears in Lamentations (1:12), "May it never occur to you!—all who pass by." Observe how, notwithstanding his own grave pain and anguish, Jeremiah did not fail to exhibit consideration for others, wishing all who pass by that they suffer no semblance of his pain and anguish. Indeed, our Rabbis of blessed memory see in this verse biblical support for the custom of saying, "May it never befall you!" (Sanhedrin 104b). Without a doubt, had they not had a compelling sensitivity toward the other, they would not have read this verse in this manner—i.e., inferring from it an injunction involving bearing the burden of the other's pain. It is, indeed, marvelous gleaning from the words of the prophets and of the Rabbis of blessed memory, the extent to which they would concern themselves with the other. How wondrous and inspiring!

As a result of my many sins, I have brought upon myself that I lack the strength to further elaborate. Thus, please recognize that the above reflects a mere drop in the sea [of all that can be said regarding our principle—namely, that whoever lacks proper manners is alien to the organism of a civilization]. I do not know the entire "sea," but from the drop that we have obtained I can assess that this matter does indeed involve a "sea" of great length and breadth!

These letters and talks of Rav Simha Zissel are compelling because they contain not a systematic and objective presentation of material, but rather the teaching voice of a living person, who continues to live in the documents we are studying. The lesson that he is trying to teach here requires elaboration. The effort of writing such a letter was difficult for Rav Simha because of the circumstances that prompted it: the student's defection. His very human voice is a tired and somewhat sad one. Yet the admission of his fatigue becomes itself the occasion for an additional teaching. In the phrase "It shouldn't happen to you," the Hebrew word *alekha* (you) can be written two different ways, with either an *alef* or an *ayin*. With an *alef* it would mean "It shouldn't happen *by* you," and with an *ayin* it would mean, "It shouldn't happen *on* you." The more common Hebrew usage would be with an *ayin,* but Rav Simḥa adopts the usage with an *alef,* which is found in the Book of Lamentations, traditionally ascribed to the prophet Jeremiah. He cites the Talmud's explanation of this usage, affirming that the phrase refers to one who, even while in great pain, is more concerned with the welfare of others than with one's own needs. Instead of crying out for help, Jeremiah therefore warns away passersby and attempts to protect them from the impending danger.

Rav Simḥa emphasizes that this behavior is characteristic of a prophet, but the tenor of the interpretation demonstrates the heightened sensitivity that the Rabbis bring to their reading. He suggests what we've called a hyperbolic or messianic horizon against which the actual letter is unfolding. Keeping hold of the vision is not the same as making the vision normative. In fact, after sharing his insight in this matter he returns to the original point, which seems to suggest that he is not a prophet. He is tired and unable to fully articulate what needs articulation. Wakefulness is a goal, not a reality. Moreover, says Rav Simḥa, even were he to achieve the ideal measure of strength, his understanding would fail him. He is merely human. No more and no less is expressed in his confession of shortcoming. And as a human being, he can only discern a drop of the sea of wisdom around him. This is, to be sure, an important drop, but it a nonetheless only a drop.

VIII   Had we already possessed no knowledge of Mussar but the contents of this letter, it would suffice us!

Having said all that, Rav Simḥa is quick to point out that were we to understand only this letter on *derekh eretz* [i.e., only chapter VII], we would have a good grounding in the essentials of Mussar.

IX   Also you, my dear, have surprised me, as you have written (words of folly, forgive me for saying) that you are envious of our friend who journeyed to Jaffa to study in isolation. I am not envious of him at all. In fact, I find it pitiful that he is acting so irresponsibly. He surely lacks a faithful comprehension of what true worship in isolation entails if, in his estimation, the place to which all of Israel [i.e., the people of Israel] had made pilgrimage is spiritually defective—and thus in its place opted for Jaffa! With wishes for your well being.

Rav Simḥa here delivers a mild rebuke. Unlike his correspondent, Rav Simḥa is not at all envious of his defecting student. The student has rejected the spiritual home of the Jewish people in favor of its physical homeland—effectively rejecting the community in favor of relative isolation from the community—and this is not enviable in Rav Simḥa's view. We should not be surprised that the decision to abandon the spiritual center of Jewish life for its ancient physical center would be looked upon with disdain by Rav Simḥa, since this was the view of many sages and community leaders, as well as of the common people, during his time. The circumstances that would transform the Jewish community in the twentieth century, leading to the establishment of the State of Israel as a crowning success for the Jewish people, still lay ahead. The political and historical underpinnings of this question are beyond the scope of this book. However, given the very different world in which we live, the central point of Rav Simḥa's teaching remains a challenge.

The rejection of the community in favor of individual pursuits—religious or otherwise—remains a central issue for contemporary Jews. For Rav Simḥa, it was inconceivable to imagine that we are free agents who could make such choice, since in his understanding we are never truly "free." We are brought into being by the community and we are indebted to it. Only in community can the burden of another be borne effectively. When we step outside there is a cost, which will need to be borne by another.

X   Addendum

Today, the third day of the week of the *Parashat Va-yechi*, the seventh day of the tenth month, I will conclude the lesson: "Whosoever Lacks Proper Manners is Alien to the Organism of a Civilization."

There is a wonderful commentary by Radak in his commentary on Jonah, regarding the prophet's escape to Tarshish. I too have always found Jonah's escape perplexing. How did he even entertain the idea of running away from God? (One should not even formulate a question with this kind of vocabulary!) Radak, quoting from a midrashic tract by our Rabbis, of blessed memory, explains Jonah's "running away" in the light of his feeling disquieted by an anticipated prophetic call to the Ninevites to repent. To be sure, Jonah was apprehensive of this prophetic call, as Gentiles are easily stirred towards repentance. He thus feared that he would have a hand in God's wrath of the Israelites, Heaven forbid, for being obdurately sinful in the face of countless prophets. Jonah, therefore, ran off abroad [i.e., outside of the boundaries of the Land of Israel, the abode of God's Glory] for, as is well known, outside of the Land of Israel a prophet cannot have a vision. Indeed, the verse itself suggests this explication. The verse says that Jonah sought to flee "from the presence of Adonai," not "from

Adonai." After all, [as in the words of the psalmist,] "Whither can I flee from You?" (Psalm 139:7).

Observe how willing Jonah was to part from the land that is delightful and good, strictly for the sake of the people of Israel [i.e., for the other]. Lo! How one ought to go to great lengths to bear the burden of another's pain—indeed, even at the price of grave and endless suffering! So much more is this duty compelling, when we consider Jonah's self-deprivation from the pleasure of prophecy, which is an endless delight. Indeed, Jonah was willing to endure anything if it benefited another! There is more to be said with regard to our discussion, but here is not the place to elaborate.

Rav Simḥa Zissel continues the theme he has been developing in the preceding letter with a second letter, attached in *Ḥokhmah U-Mussar* to that previous letter. This second letter is actually dated and is obviously a follow-up, and so is included in the same chapter.

The idea of the student's flight from his home community apparently reminds Rav Simḥa of the flight of Jonah, who attempted to escape from God and the responsibility to prophesy to the people of Nineveh. The question he begins with is one that always troubled him: How is it possible to even conceive of a flight from God? Aside from being an impossibility, to the extent that one thinks one is fleeing from God, one is clearly fleeing from the responsibility of bearing the burden of another. But Rav Simḥa finds a comment by the biblical commentator Radak (Rabbi David Kimḥi) that explains the meaning of this flight and, in doing so, casts it in a much more positive light than we might expect.

According to Radak, Jonah fled from his responsibility because he was aware that he would be believed. Since Gentiles would be more likely to repent than Israelites, the repentance of the Ninevites would then place the refusal of Israelites to repent, either in

Jonah's own time or in any other time, in a much harsher light. Thus, Jonah's flight was occasioned by his obsessive concern for the harm that would come to the people of Israel, by the punishment they would suffer for refusing to repent—a punishment made all the more harsh in light of the ease with which the Gentiles accepted the word of a prophet, compared to the stubbornness of the Israelites who turn a deaf ear to prophet after prophet. The physical flight of Jonah is from the Land of Israel. Leaving Israel is considered to be a significant sacrifice on the part of the prophet, since it would entail a cessation of his prophecy. Yet, Jonah was willing to make such a sacrifice because of his obsession to bear the burden of Israel's suffering, even their future suffering.

In what way does this "addendum" impact the lesson that Simha Zissel has elaborated in this chapter? At first glance we might conclude that he has decided to defend the notion of flight, thereby softening his condemnation of his student. But this is not the case; Rav Simha is making precisely the opposite point. The prophet leaves the Land (and the presence of God) in order to bear the burden of his people. The attraction of the Land—which has perhaps "better access" to the presence of God—does not take precedence over one's responsibility toward others, toward the community. Rav Simha acknowledges that his student is seeking the presence of God by escaping to the Land, he acknowledges that in the conventional religious scheme of things this might appear laudatory, but he is asserting that seeking personal religious satisfaction in this way is misdirected. It constitutes a misreading of what religious life is about. One who substitutes the presence of God for the responsibility of bearing the burden of his neighbor has missed the point of religious life.

In passing, this "addendum" raises other issues that might be of interest—the relative differences between Jews and Gentiles regarding of the willingness to repent, for example. Does this tell us something about the view of non-Jews in Rav Simḥa's world? What are we to make of this characterization of Jews as almost immune to repentance? While others may want to use this text to delve into questions of history, our goal remains to stay with the Mussar of Rav Simḥa. As Rav Simḥa wrote: "There is much more to be said with regard to our discussion, but here is not the place to elaborate."

Bibliography

Works by Emmanuel Levinas

Alterity & Transcendence. Translated by Michael B. Smith. Columbia University Press, 1999.

Basic Philosophical Writings. Edited by Adriaan T. Peperzak, Simon Critchley, and Robert Bernasconi. Indiana University Press, 1996.

Beyond the Verse: Talmudic Readings and Lectures. Translated by Gary D. Mole. Indiana University Press, 1994.

Collected Philosophical Papers. Translated by Alphonso Lingis. Martinus Nijhoff/The Hague, 1987.

Difficult Freedom: Essays on Judaism. Translated by Sean Hand. The Johns Hopkins University Press, 1990.

Discovering Existence with Husserl. Translated and edited by Richard A. Cohen and Michael B. Smith. Northwestern University Press, 1998.

Entre Nous: On Thinking of the Other. Translated by Michael B. Smith and Barbara Harshav. Columbia University Press, 1998.

Ethics and Infinity. Translated by Richard A. Cohen. Duquesne University Press, 1985.

Existence and Existents. Translated by Alphonso Lingis. Martinus Nijhoff/The Hague, 1978.

God, Death, and Time. Translated by Bettina Bergo. Stanford University Press, 2000.

Humanism of the Other. Translated by Nidra Poller. University of Illinois Press, 2003.

In the Time of the Nations. Translated by Michael B. Smith. Indiana University Press, 1994.

New Talmudic Readings. Translated by Richard A. Cohen. Duquesne University Press, 1999.

Nine Talmudic Readings. Translated by Annette Aronowicz. Indiana University Press, 1990.

Of God Who Comes to Mind. Translated by Bettina Bergo. Stanford University Press, 1998.

On Escape. Translated by Bettina Bergo. Stanford University Press, 2003.

Otherwise Than Being or Beyond Essence. Translated by Alphonso Lingis. Kluwer Academic Publishers, 1991.

Outside the Subject. Translated by Michael B. Smith. Stanford University Press, 1994.

Proper Names. Translated by Michael B. Smith. Stanford University Press, 1996.

The Theory of Intuition in Husserl's Phenomenology. Translated by André Orianne. Northwestern University Press, 1993.

Time and the Other. Translated by Richard A. Cohen. Duquesne University Press, 1987.

Totality and Infinity. Translated by Alphonso Lingis. Duquesne University Press, 1969.

Unforeseen History. Translated by Nidra Poller. University of Illinois Press, 2004.

Secondary Sources—Emmanuel Levinas

Ajzenstate, Oona. *Driven Back to the Text.* Duquesne University Press, 2001.

Bernasconi, Robert and David Wood. *The Provocation of Levinas: Rethinking the Other.* Routledge, 1988.

Chanter, Tina. *Feminist Interpretations of Emmanuel Levinas.* The Pennsylvania State University Press, 2001.

Cohen, Richard A. *Elevations: The Height of the Good in Rosenzweig and Levinas.* The University of Chicago Press, 1994.

_____. *Ethics, Exegesis, and Philosophy.* Cambridge University Press, 2001.

_____. *Face to Face With Levinas.* State University of New York Press, 1986.

Gibbs, Robert. *Correlations in Rosenzweig and Levinas.* Princeton University Press, 1992.

Handelman, Susan A. *Fragments of Redemption.* Indiana University Press, 1991.

Katz, Claire Elise. *Levinas, Judaism, and the Feminine.* Indiana University Press, 2003.

Kosky, Jeffrey L. *Levinas and the Philosophy of Religion.* Indiana University Press, 2001.

Llewelyn, John. *Emmanuel Levinas: The Genealogy of Ethics.* Routledge, 1995.

Peperzak, Adriaan. *To the Other: An Introduction to the Philosophy of Emmanuel Levinas.* Purdue University Press, 1993.

Robbins, Jill. *Is It Righteous To Be? Interviews with Emmanuel Levinas.* Stanford University Press, 2001.

Stone, Ira F. *Reading Levinas/Reading Talmud.* The Jewish Publication Society, 1998.

Wyschogrod, Edith. *Emmanuel Levinas: The Problem of Ethical Metaphysics.* Fordham University Press, 2000.

Mussar Primary Sources

Cordovero, Rabbi Moshe. *The Palm Tree of Devorah.* Translated by Rabbi Moshe Miller. Targum Press Inc., 1993.

Luzzatto, Moshe Chayim. *Mesillat Yesharim: The Path of the Just.* Translated by Shraga Silverstein. Feldheim Publishers, 1969.

_____. *Mesillat Yesharim: The Path of the Upright.* Translated and edited by Mordecai M. Kaplan. The Jewish Publication Society, 1966.

_____. *Mesillat Yesharim L'or Kitvei HaRamhal.* Machon Ramhal, Jerusalem.

_____. *The Knowing Heart.* English translation by Shraga Silverstein, Feldheim Publishers, 1982.

_____. *The Way of God.* Translated by Aryeh Kaplan. Feldheim Publishers, 1983.

Paquda, R. Bahya ben Joseph ibn. *Duties of the Heart.* Translated by R. Yehudah ibn Tibbon. Feldheim Publishers, 1996.

Salanter, Rabbi Israel. *Ohr Yisrael Vol 1,* in *Me'orei Orot Ha-mussar.* Moriah Offset Co., Brooklyn, NY.

_____. *Ohr Yisrael: The Classic Writings of Rav Yisrael Salanter and His Disciple Rav Yitzchak Blazer.* Translated by Rabbi Zvi Miller; edited by Rabbi Eli Linas. Targum Press, 2004.

Satanov, Rabbi Mendel of. *Heshbon Ha-nefesh.* Based on a translation by Shraga Silverstein. Feldheim Publishers, 1995.

Twerski, Rabbi Abraham J. *Lights Along the Way.* Mesorah Publications, Ltd. 1995.

Zissel, Rav Simha of Kelm. *Hokhmah U-Mussar,* volumes 2 & 3 in *Me'orei Orot HaMussar 1964.* Rabbi Simcha Ziesel Levovitz, Publisher, Brooklyn, NY.

Kitvei Ha-saba Ve-talmidav Mi-Kelm, Siftei Hakhamin. Institute for the Dissemination of Torah and Mussar.

Mussar Secondary Sources

Bindman, Yirmeyahu. *Rabbi Moshe Chaim Luzzatto: His Life and Works.* Jason Aronson, Inc., 1995.

Eckman, Lester Samuel. *The History of the Mussar Movement 1840–1945.* Shengold Publishers, Inc.

Etkes, Immanuel. *Rabbi Israel Salanter and the Mussar Movement: Seeking the Torah of Truth.* The Jewish Publication Society, 1993.

Goldberg, Hillel. *Israel Salanter: Text, Structure, Idea.* Ktav Publishing House Inc., 1992.

_____. *The Musar Anthology.* 1972. Free distribution to Jewish students in Boston and New York aided by Jewish Student Projects and Jewish Association for College Youth.

Katz, Rabbi Dov. *The Mussar Movement: Its History, Leading Personalities, and Doctrines.* Orly Press, 1977.

_____. *Tenuat Ha-mussar.* A. Gitter (Jerusalem), 1982.

Levin, Meir. *Novarodok: A Movement That Lived in Struggle and Its Unique Approach to the Problem of Man.* Jason Aronson, Inc., 1996.

Morinis, Alan. *Climbing Jacob's Ladder: One Man's Rediscovery of a Jewish Spiritual Tradition.* Random House/Broadway Books, 2002.

Shafronsky, Avrohom Zelik. *Some Gems from the Mind of the Alter of Novardok.* Torah Award Fund, 1979.

Ury, Dr. Zalman F. *Studies in Torah Judaism: The Mussar Movement.* Yeshiva University Press, 1970.

General Bibliography

Batnitzky, Leora. *Idolatry and Representation: The Philosophy of Franz Rosenzweig Reconsidered.* Princeton University Press, 2000.

Buber, Martin. *I and Thou.* Scribner Classic/Collier Edition, 1987.

Derrida, Jacques. *Adieu to Emmanuel Levinas.* Translated by Pascale-Anne Brault and Michael Naas. Stanford University Press, 1999.

Fishbane, Michael. *The Garments of Torah.* Indiana University Press, 1992.

Heschel, Abraham Joshua. *God in Search of Man.* Jason Aronson, Inc., 1987.

Kaplan, Edward K. *Holiness in Words: Abraham Joshua Heschel's Poetics of Piety.* State University of New York Press, 1996.

Kepnes, Steven. *Interpreting Judaism in a Postmodern Age.* New York University Press, 1996.

Lamm, Norman. *Torah Lishmah: Torah for Torah's Sake.* Ktav Publishing House, Inc., 1989.

Ochs, Peter and Levene, Nancy. *Textual Reasoning.* Wm. B. Eerdmans Publishing Co., 2003.

Perlman, Lawrence. *Abraham Heschel's Idea of Revelation.* Brown University, 1989.

Rosenzweig, Franz. *The Star of Redemption.* Translated by William W. Hallo. Notre Dame Press, 1985.

_____. *The New Thinking.* Translated and edited by Alan Udoff and Barbara E. Galli. Syracuse University Press, 1999.